Instrument Oral Exam Guide

Fourth Edition

The comprehensive
guide to prepare you
for the FAA Oral Exam

by Michael D. Hayes

Aviation Supplies & Academics, Inc.
Newcastle, Washington

Instrument Oral Exam Guide
Fourth Edition

Aviation Supplies & Academics, Inc.
7005 132nd Place SE
Newcastle, Washington 98059-3153

Printed in the United States of America

01   00   99   9   8   7   6   5   4   3   2

ISBN 1-56027-318-6
ASA-OEG-I4

This guide is dedicated to the many talented students, pilots and flight instructors I have had the opportunity to work with over the years. Also, special thanks to Mark Hayes, Robert Hess, Meredyth Malocsay, and many others who supplied the patience, encouragement, and understanding necessary to complete the project.

— M.D.H.

Contents

Continued

Introduction

The *Instrument Oral Exam Guide* is a comprehensive guide designed for private or commercial pilots who are involved in training for the instrument rating. This guide was originally designed for use in a Part 141 flight school, but quickly became popular with those training under 14 CFR Part 61 not affiliated with an approved school. The guide will also prove beneficial to instrument-rated pilots who wish to refresh their knowledge or are preparing for an instrument competency check.

The guide is divided into four main sections which represent logical divisions of a typical instrument flight. An FAA examiner may ask questions from any of the subject areas within these divisions, at any time during the practical test, to determine if the applicant has the required knowledge. Through intensive post-instrument-checkride debriefings, we have provided you with the most consistent questions asked along with the information necessary for a knowledgeable response.

You may supplement this guide with other study materials as noted in parentheses after each question; for example: (AC 61-27C). The abbreviations for these materials and their titles are listed below. Be sure that you use the latest revision of these references when reviewing for the test.

14 CFR Part 61	*Certification: Pilots and Flight Instructors*
14 CFR Part 91	*General Operating and Flight Rules*
AC 61-27C	*Instrument Flying Handbook*
AIM	*Aeronautical Information Manual*
AC 61-23C	*Pilot's Handbook of Aeronautical Knowledge*
AC 00-6A	*Aviation Weather*
AC 00-45D	*Aviation Weather Services*

All the books listed above are reprinted by ASA and are available from aviation retailers nationwide.

Continued

AC 00-54   *Pilot Windshear Guide*
AC 90-94   *Guidelines for Using GPS Equipment*

These Advisory Circulars are available free from the Government Printing Office.

A review of the information presented within this guide should provide the necessary preparation for the oral section of an FAA instrument certification or re-certification check.

Flight Planning

1

A. Certificates, Ratings and Currency Requirements

1. An applicant for an instrument rating must have at least how much and what type of flight time as pilot?
(14 CFR 61.65)

An applicant must have:

a. 50 hours of cross-country flight time as PIC, of which at least 10 hours must be in airplanes;

b. 40 hours of actual or simulated instrument time (on the areas of operation specified);

c. 15 hours of instrument flight training from an authorized instructor in the aircraft category for which the instrument rating is sought;

d. 3 hours of instrument training appropriate to the instrument rating sought from an authorized instructor, in preparation for the practical test, within the 60 days preceding the date of test.

2. When is an instrument rating required?
(14 CFR 61.3e, 91.157)

When operations are conducted:

a. Under instrument flight rules (IFR flight plan),

b. In weather conditions less than the minimum for VFR flight,

c. In Class A airspace,

d. Under Special VFR within Class B, Class C, Class D and Class E surface areas between sunset and sunrise.

3. **What are the recency-of-experience requirements to be PIC of a flight under IFR?** (14 CFR 61.57)

   The recency-of-experience requirements are:

   a. A biennial flight review;

   b. To carry passengers, 3 takeoffs and landings within the preceding 90 days (full stop at night);

   c. Within the preceding 6 calendar months, logged under actual or simulated instrument conditions, either in flight in the appropriate category of aircraft, or in a flight simulator or flight training device (representative of the category for the privileges sought)—

      i. At least six instrument approaches;

      ii. Holding procedures; and

      iii. Intercepting and tracking courses through the use of navigation systems.

4. **If a pilot allows his/her instrument currency to expire, what can be done to become current again?** (14 CFR 61.57)

   A pilot is current for the first 6 months following his/her instrument checkride or proficiency check. If the pilot has not accomplished at least 6 approaches (including holding procedures, intercepting/tracking courses through the use of navigation systems) within this first 6 months, he/she is no longer legal to file and fly under IFR. To become legal again, the regulations allow a "grace period" (the second 6-month period), in which a pilot may get current by finding an "appropriately rated" safety pilot, and in simulated IFR conditions only, acquire the 6 approaches, etc. If the second 6-month period also passes without accomplishing the minimum, a pilot may reinstate his/her currency by accomplishing an instrument proficiency check given by an examiner, an authorized instructor, or an FAA-approved person to conduct instrument practical tests.

5. Define "appropriately rated safety pilot." (14 CFR 91.109)

This person must hold at least a Private Pilot certificate. They must also have a current medical certificate and be current in the category and class of aircraft being flown (i.e., airplane single-engine land). This person need not be instrument rated.

B. Preflight Action for Flight
(IFR or Flight Not in the Vicinity of Airport)

1. What information must a pilot-in-command be familiar with before a flight? (14 CFR 91.103)

All available information including:

a. Weather reports and forecasts

b. Fuel requirements

c. Alternatives if the flight cannot be completed as planned

d. Known ATC delays

e. Runway lengths of intended use

f. Takeoff and landing distances

2. What are the fuel requirements for flight in IFR conditions? (14 CFR 91.167)

The aircraft must carry enough fuel to fly to the first airport of intended landing (including the approach), the alternate airport (if required), and thereafter, for 45 minutes at normal cruise power. If an alternate airport is not required, enough fuel must be carried to fly to the destination airport and land with 45 minutes of fuel remaining.

C. Preflight Action for Aircraft

1. Who is responsible for determining if an aircraft is in an airworthy condition? (14 CFR 91.7)

The pilot-in-command is responsible.

2. What aircraft instruments/equipment are required for IFR operations? (14 CFR 91.205)

Those required for VFR day and night flight plus:

G enerator or alternator of adequate capacity

R adios (appropriate for facilities used)

A ltimeter (sensitive)

B all (slip/skid indicator of turn coordinator)

C lock (sweep second hand or digital presentation)

A ttitude Indicator

R ate of Turn (turn coordinator)

D irectional Gyro

3. What are the required tests and inspections of aircraft and equipment to be legal for IFR flight? (14 CFR 91.171, 91.409, 91.411 and 91.413)

a. The aircraft must have an annual inspection. If operated for hire or rental, it must also have a 100-hour inspection. A record must be kept in the aircraft/engine logbooks.

b. The pitot/static system must have been checked within the preceding 24 calendar months. A record must be kept in the aircraft logbook.

c. The transponder must have been checked within the preceding 24 calendar months. A record must be kept in the aircraft logbook.

d. The altimeter must have been checked within the preceding 24 calendar months. A record must be kept in the aircraft logbook.

e. The VOR must have been checked within the preceding 30 days. A record must be kept in a bound logbook.

4. May portable electronic devices be operated onboard an aircraft? (14 CFR 91.21)

No person may operate nor may any PIC allow the operation of any portable electronic device:

a. On aircraft operated by an air carrier or commercial operator; or

b. On any other aircraft while it is operated under IFR.

Exceptions are: portable voice recorders, hearing aids, heart pacemakers, electric shavers or any other portable electronic device that the operator of the aircraft has determined will not cause interference with the navigation or communication system of the aircraft.

5. What documents must be onboard an aircraft to make it legal for IFR flight? (14 CFR 91.203)

a. Airworthiness Certificate

b. Registration Certificate

c. Owner's manual or operating limitations

d. Weight and balance data

D. IFR Flight Plan

1. When must a pilot file an IFR flight plan? (AIM 5-1-7)

Prior to departure from within or prior to entering controlled airspace, a pilot must submit a complete flight plan and receive clearance from ATC if weather conditions are below VFR minimums. The pilot should file the flight plan at least 30 minutes prior to the estimated time of departure to preclude a possible delay in receiving a departure clearance from ATC.

2. When can you cancel your IFR flight plan? (AIM 5-1-13)

An IFR flight plan may be canceled at any time the flight is operating in VFR conditions outside of Class A airspace. Pilots must be aware that other procedures may be applicable to a flight

Continued

that cancels an IFR flight plan within an area where a special program, such as a designated TRSA, Class C airspace, or Class B airspace, has been established.

3. What is a composite flight plan? (AIM 5-1-6)

It is a flight plan that specifies VFR operation for one portion of a flight, and IFR for another.

4. What four pieces of equipment determine your "special equipment" suffix when filing an IFR flight plan? (AIM 5-1-7)

a. Radar beacon transponder

b. DME equipment

c. TACAN only equipment

d. RNAV

Note: Equipment suffixes also exist for GPS and Flight Management Systems. Criteria for use of these designators are presently identified only for certain RNAV-equipped aircraft and qualified pilots.

5. The requested altitude on an FAA flight plan form (Block 7) represents which altitude for the route of flight—the initial, lowest, or highest? (AIM 5-1-7)

Enter only the initial requested altitude in this block. When more than one IFR altitude or flight level is desired along the route of flight, it is best to make a subsequent request direct to the controller.

6. What are the alternate airport requirements? (14 CFR 91.169c)

1-2-3 Rule—If from 1 hour before to 1 hour after your planned ETA at the destination airport, the weather is forecast to be at least 2,000-foot ceilings and/or 3-mile visibilities, no alternate is required. If less than 2,000 and/or 3 miles, an alternate must be filed using the following criteria:

    a. If an IAP is published for that airport, the alternate airport minimums specified in that procedure or, if none are specified, the following minimums—

        i. Precision approach procedure: ceiling 600 feet and visibility 2 statute miles.

        ii. Nonprecision approaches: ceiling 800 feet and visibility 2 statute miles.

    b. If no IAP has been published for that airport, the ceiling and visibility minimums are those allowing descent from the MEA, approach, and landing under basic VFR.

7. What is the definition of the term "ceiling"?
(Pilot/Controller Glossary)

Ceiling is defined as the height above the earth's surface of the lowest layer of clouds or obscuring phenomena reported as "broken," "overcast," or "obscuration," and not classified as "thin" or "partial."

8. What minimums are to be used on arrival at the alternate? (14 CFR 91.169c)

If an instrument approach procedure has been published for that airport, the minimums specified in that procedure are used.

E. Route Planning

1. What are preferred routes and where can they be found?
(Pilot/Controller Glossary)

Preferred routes are those established between busier airports to increase system efficiency and capacity. Preferred routes are listed in the Airport/Facility Directory.

2. What are Enroute Low-Altitude Charts? (AIM 9-1-4)

Enroute low-altitude charts provide aeronautical information for navigation under IFR conditions below 18,000 feet MSL. These charts are revised every 56 days.

3. How often are Enroute Low-Altitude Charts published? (AIM 9-1-4)

They are published every 56 days.

4. What are "area charts"? (AIM 9-1-4)

Area charts furnish terminal information at a large scale in congested areas such as Dallas/Ft.Worth, Atlanta, etc. Multiple area charts are printed in one publication and are revised every 56 days.

5. Where can information on possible navigational aid limitations be found? (AIM 9-1-4)

The Airport/Facility Directory.

6. What other useful information can be found in the Airport/Facility Directory which might be helpful in route planning? (A/FD)

The Airport/Facility Directory contains additional information for each of the seven regions covered, such as:

a. Enroute Flight Advisory Services — locations and communications outlets.

b. ARTCC — locations and sector frequencies.

c. Aeronautical Chart Bulletins — recent changes after publication.

d. Preferred IFR routes — high and low altitude.

e. Special notices — flight service station, GADO, Weather Service office phone numbers.

f. VOR receiver checkpoints — locations and frequencies.

7. What are NOTAMs? (AIM 5-1-3)

Notices To Airmen (NOTAM)—Time critical aeronautical information, which is of either a temporary nature or not known sufficiently in advance to permit publication on aeronautical charts or in other operational publications, receives immediate dissemination via the National NOTAM System. It is aeronautical information that could affect a pilot's decision to make a flight. It includes such information as airport or primary runway closures, changes in the status of navigational aids, ILS's, radar service availability, and other information essential to planned en route, terminal, or landing operations.

8. What are the three categories of NOTAMs? (AIM 5-1-3)

There are three types of NOTAMs generated by the FAA:

a. *NOTAM (D)*—A NOTAM given (in addition to local) distant dissemination beyond the area of responsibility of the Flight Service Station. These NOTAMs will be stored and available until canceled. NOTAM (D)s contain information on all civil public use airports and navigational facilities that are part of the National Airspace System. NOTAM (D) items are serious enough to affect the usability of an airport or a certain facility.

b. *NOTAM (L)*—A NOTAM given local dissemination by voice and other means to satisfy local user requirements. NOTAM (L) information may cover items such as taxiway closures, persons and/or equipment near or crossing runways, airport rotating beacon outages, and other information that would have little impact on non-local operations.

c. *FDC NOTAM*—The National Flight Data Center will issue these NOTAMs when it becomes necessary to disseminate information which is regulatory in nature. FDC NOTAMs contain items such as amendments to published IAPs and other current aeronautical charts. They are also used to advertise temporary flight restrictions caused by natural disasters or large scale public events that may generate congestion of air traffic over a site.

9. **Which type of NOTAMs will be omitted from a pilot briefing, if not specifically requested by the pilot?** (AIM 7-1-3)

   NOTAM (D) information and FDC NOTAMs that have been published in the Notices to Airmen publication are not included in pilot briefings unless a review of this publication is specifically requested by the pilot. For complete flight information, review the printed NOTAMs in the Notices to Airmen publication and the Airport/Facility Directory, in addition to obtaining a briefing.

10. **Where can NOTAM information be obtained?** (AIM 5-1-3)

    a. Nearest FSS
    b. Airport/Facility Directory
    c. Locally broadcast ATIS
    d. Hourly surface observations
    e. Notices to Airmen publication (NTAP) — Printed NOTAMs; these are not normally provided in a briefing, and pilots must make specific requests for them.

F. Aircraft Systems

Pitot/Static System

1. **What instruments operate from the pitot/static system?** (AC 61-27C, Ch. 4)

   The pitot/static system operates the altimeter, vertical-speed indicator, and airspeed indicator.

2. **How does an altimeter work?** (AC 61-27C, Ch. 4)

   In an altimeter, aneroid wafers expand and contract as atmospheric pressure changes, and through a shaft and gear linkage, rotate pointers on the dial of the instrument.

3. What are the limitations that a pressure altimeter is subject to? (AC 61-27C, Ch. 4)

Nonstandard pressure and temperature:

a. Temperature variations expand or contract the atmosphere and raise or lower pressure levels that the altimeter senses.

   On a warm day—The pressure level is higher than on a standard day. The altimeter indicates lower than actual altitude.

   On a cold day—The pressure level is lower than on a standard day. The altimeter indicates higher than actual altitude.

b. Changes in surface pressure also affect pressure levels at altitude.

   Higher than standard pressure—The pressure level is higher than on a standard day. The altimeter indicates lower than actual altitude.

   Lower than standard pressure—The pressure level is lower than on a standard day. The altimeter indicates higher than actual altitude.

   Remember: High to low or hot to cold look out below!

4. For IFR flight, what is the maximum allowable error for an altimeter? (AC 61-27C, Ch. 4)

If the altimeter is off field elevation by more than 75 feet, with the correct pressure set in the Kollsman window, it is considered to be unreliable.

5. Define and state how you determine the following altitudes:

Indicated altitude	**Density altitude**
Pressure altitude	**Absolute altitude**
True altitude	

(AC 61-27C, Ch. 4)

Indicated altitude—Read off the face of the altimeter.

Pressure altitude—Indicated altitude with 29.92" Hg set in the Kollsman window.

Continued

True altitude—Height above sea level. Use the flight computer.

Density altitude—Pressure altitude corrected for non-standard temperature. Use the flight computer.

Absolute altitude—Height above ground. Subtract the terrain elevation from true altitude.

6. How does the airspeed indicator operate?
(AC 61-27C, Ch. 4)

The airspeed indicator measures the difference between ram pressure from the pitot head and atmospheric pressure from the static source.

7. What are the limitations the airspeed indicator is subject to? (AC 61-27C, Ch. 4)

It must have proper flow of air in the pitot/static system.

8. What are the errors that the airspeed indicator is subject to? (AC 61-27C, Ch. 4)

Position error—Caused by the static ports sensing erroneous static pressure; slipstream flow causes disturbances at the static port preventing actual atmospheric pressure measurement. It varies with airspeed, altitude, configuration and may be a plus or minus value.

Density error—Changes in altitude and temperature are not compensated for by the instrument.

Compressibility error—Caused by the packing of air into the pitot tube at high airspeeds, resulting in higher than normal indications. It usually occurs above 180 KIAS.

9. What are the different types of aircraft speeds?
(AC 61-27C, Ch. 4)

Indicated airspeed—Read off the instrument.

Calibrated airspeed—IAS corrected for instrument and position errors; obtained from the manual or off the face of the instrument.

Equivalent airspeed—CAS corrected for adiabatic compressible flow at altitude.

True airspeed—CAS corrected for non-standard temperature and pressure; obtained from the flight computer, manual, or the A/S indicator slide computer.

Groundspeed—TAS corrected for wind; speed across the ground; use the flight computer.

10. Are the color bands on an airspeed indicator indicated airspeeds or calibrated airspeeds?

Airspeed indicators indicate CAS (usually in mph) if manufactured in 1975 or before, and IAS (usually in knots) if manufactured in 1976 or after.

11. How does the vertical-speed indicator work?
(AC 61-27C, Ch. 4)

In the VSI, changing pressures expand or contract a diaphragm connected to the indicating needle through gears and levers. The VSI is connected to the static pressure line through a calibrated leak; it measures differential pressure.

12. What are the limitations of the vertical-speed indicator?
(AC 61-27C, Ch. 4)

It is not accurate until the aircraft is stabilized. Sudden or abrupt changes in the aircraft attitude will cause erroneous instrument readings as airflow fluctuates over the static port. These changes are not reflected immediately by the VSI due to the calibrated leak.

13. What instruments are affected when the pitot tube freezes? (AC 61-27C, Ch. 4)

Only the airspeed indicator will be affected. It acts like an altimeter—it will read higher as the aircraft climbs and lower as the aircraft descends. It reads lower than actual speed in level flight.

14. What instruments are affected when the static port freezes? (AC 61-27C, Ch. 4)

Airspeed indicator—Accurate at the altitude frozen as long as static pressure in the indicator and the system equals outside pressure. If the aircraft descends, the airspeed indicator would read high (outside static pressure would be greater than that trapped). If the aircraft climbs, the airspeed indicator would read low.

Altimeter—Indicates the altitude at which the system is blocked.

Vertical speed—Will indicate level flight.

15. If the air temperature is +6°C at an airport elevation of 1,200 feet and a standard (average) temperature lapse rate exists, what will be the approximate freezing level?

4,200 MSL; 6° at the surface divided by the average temperature lapse rate of 2°C results in a 3,000-foot freezing level, converted to sea level by adding the 1,200-foot airport elevation.

16. What corrective action is needed if the pitot tube freezes? If the static port freezes? (AC 61-27C, Ch. 4)

For pitot tube—Turn pitot heat on.

For static system—Use alternate air if available or break the face of a static instrument (either the VSI or A/S indicator).

17. What indications should you expect while using alternate air? (AC 61-27C, Ch. 4)

In many unpressurized aircraft equipped with a pitot-static tube, an alternate source of static pressure is provided for emergency use. If the alternate source is vented inside the airplane, where static pressure is usually lower than outside, selection of the alternate static source may result in the following instrument indications:

Altimeter..reads higher than normal
Airspeed indicator ....indicated airspeed reads
                                                              greater than normal
Vertical velocity indicator ....momentarily shows a climb

Vacuum/Gyroscopic System

1. What instruments operate from the vacuum system?
(AC 61-27C, Ch. 4)

Normally the attitude indicator and directional gyro rely on the vacuum system for operation. The turn coordinator could also be vacuum-driven depending on the particular aircraft. The industry standard dictates that the artificial horizon and directional gyro be vacuum-driven and the turn coordinator be electrically-driven. However, in some systems, all three can be electrically-driven.

2. How does the vacuum system operate?
(AC 61-27C, Ch. 4)

An engine-driven vacuum pump provides suction which pulls air from the instrument case. Normal pressure entering the case is directed against rotor vanes to turn the rotor (gyro) at high speed, much like a water wheel or turbine operates. Air is drawn into the instrument through a filter from the cockpit and eventually vented outside. Vacuum values vary but provide rotor speeds from 8,000 to 18,000 RPM.

3. How does the attitude indicator work? (AC 61-27C, Ch. 4)

A gyro stabilizes the artificial horizon parallel to the real horizon in the attitude indicator.

4. What are the limitations of an attitude indicator?
(AC 61-27C, Ch. 4)

The pitch-and-bank limits depend upon the make and model of the instrument. Limits in the banking plane are usually from 100 degrees to 110 degrees, and the pitch limits are usually from 60 to 70 degrees. If either limit is exceeded, the instrument will tumble or spill, and will give incorrect indications until reset. A number of modern attitude indicators will not tumble.

5. What are the errors that the attitude indicator is subject to? (AC 61-27C, Ch. 4)

Errors in both pitch and bank occur during normal coordinated turns. These errors are caused by the movement of pendulous vanes by centrifugal force, resulting in precession of the gyro toward the inside of the turn. The greatest error occurs in 180 degrees of turn. In a 180-degree turn to the right, on rollout the attitude indicator will indicate a slight climb and turn to the left. Acceleration and deceleration errors cause the attitude indicator to indicate a climb when the aircraft is accelerated and a descent when the aircraft is decelerated.

6. How does the directional gyro operate? (AC 61-27C, Ch. 4)

A gyro stabilizes the heading indicator. The speed of the gyro is usually 10,000 to 18,000 RPM.

7. What are the limitations of the directional gyro? (AC 61-27C, Ch. 4)

The pitch-and-bank limits of the heading indicator vary with the particular design and make of instrument. On some heading indicators found in light airplanes, the limits are approximately 55 degrees of pitch and 55 degrees of bank. When either of these attitude limits is exceeded, the instrument "tumbles" or "spills" and no longer gives the correct indication until reset. After spilling, it may be reset with the caging knob. Many of the modern instruments used are designed in such a manner that they will not tumble.

8. What are the errors that the directional gyro is subject to? (AC 61-27C, Ch. 4)

It is subject to precession of the gyro. Maximum allowable precession is 3° in 15 minutes.

Electric/Gyroscopic System

1. What instruments operate on the electric/gyroscopic system? (AC 61-27C, Ch. 4)

Turn coordinator—This system could also operate the artificial horizon and directional gyro, depending on the particular aircraft (refer to vacuum/gyro system question #1).

2. How does the turn coordinator operate? (AC 61-27C, Ch. 4)

The turn part of the instrument uses precession to indicate direction and approximate rate of turn. A gyro reacts by trying to move in reaction to the force applied, thus moving the needle or miniature aircraft in proportion to the rate of turn. The slip/skid indicator is a liquid-filled tube with a ball that reacts to centrifugal force and gravity.

3. What information does the turn coordinator provide? (AC 61-27C, Ch. 4)

The miniature aircraft of the turn coordinator displays the rate of turn and rate of roll. The ball in the tube indicates a slipping or skidding condition.

Slip—ball on the inside of turn; not enough rate of turn for the amount of bank.

Skid—ball to the outside of turn; too much rate of turn for the amount of bank.

4. What limitations apply to the turn coordinator? (AC 61-27C, Ch. 4)

A spring is attached between the instrument case and the gyro assembly to hold the gyro upright when no precession force is applied. Tension on the spring may be adjusted to calibrate the instrument for a given rate of turn. The spring restricts the amount of gyro tilt. Stops prevent the gyro assembly from tilting more than 45 degrees to either side of the upright position.

Magnetic Compass

1. How does the magnetic compass work?
(AC 61-27C, Ch. 4)

Magnets mounted on the compass card align themselves parallel to the earth's lines of magnetic force.

2. What limitations does the magnetic compass have?
(AC 61-27C, Ch. 4)

The float assembly of the compass is balanced on a pivot, which allows free rotation of the card and allows it to tilt at an angle up to 18 degrees.

3. What are the various compass errors?
(AC 61-27C, Ch. 4)

Oscillation error—Erratic movement of the compass card caused by turbulence or rough control technique.

Deviation error—Due to electrical and magnetic disturbances in the aircraft.

Variation error—Angular difference between true and magnetic north; reference isogonic lines of variation.

Dip errors:

a. *Acceleration error*—On east or west headings, while accelerating, the magnetic compass shows a turn to the north, and when decelerating, it shows a turn to the south.

   Remember: ANDS
   A ccelerate
   N orth
   D ecelerate
   S outh

b. *Northerly turning error*— The compass leads in the south half of a turn, and lags in the north half of a turn.

Remember: UNOS
U ndershoot
N orth
O vershoot
S outh

G. Fundamentals of Weather

1. **At what rate does atmospheric pressure decrease with an increase in altitude?** (AC 00-6A)

Atmospheric pressure decreases approximately 1" Hg per 1,000 feet.

2. **What are the standard temperature and pressure values for sea level?** (AC 00-6A)

15°C and 29.92" Hg are standard at sea level.

3. **State the general characteristics in regard to the flow of air around high and low pressure systems in the northern hemisphere.** (AC 00-6A)

Low pressure— Air flows inward, upward, and counterclockwise.
High pressure— Air flows outward, downward, and clockwise.

4. **What causes the winds aloft to flow parallel to the isobars?** (AC 00-6A)

The Coriolis force causes winds aloft to flow parallel to the isobars.

5. **Why do surface winds generally flow across the isobars at an angle?** (AC 00-6A)

Surface friction causes winds to flow across isobars at an angle.

6. When temperature and dew point are close together (within 5°), what type of weather is likely? (AC 00-6A)

Visible moisture is likely, in the form of clouds, dew or fog.

7. What factor primarily determines the type and vertical extent of clouds? (AC 00-6A)

The stability of the atmosphere determines type and vertical extent of clouds.

8. What is the difference between a stable and an unstable atmosphere? (AC 00-6A)

An unstable atmosphere is one in which, if air is displaced vertically, it will continue to move vertically; a stable atmosphere is one which tends to resist any vertical movement of air.

9. How do you determine the stability of the atmosphere? (AC 00-6A)

By observing the actual lapse rate and comparing it to the standard lapse rate of 3.5°F per 1,000 feet. The "K" index of a stability chart is the primary means of determining stability.

10. List the effects of stable and unstable air on clouds, turbulence, precipitation and visibility. (AC 00-6A)

	Stable	Unstable
Clouds	Stratiform	Cumuliform
Turbulence	Smooth	Rough
Precipitation	Steady	Showery
Visibility	Fair to Poor	Good

11. What are the two main types of icing? (AC 00-6A)

Structural and induction are the two main types of icing.

12. Name four types of structural ice. (AC 00-6A)

Clear ice—Forms when large drops strike the aircraft surface and slowly freeze.

Rime ice—Small drops strike the aircraft and freeze rapidly.

Mixed ice—Combination of the above; supercooled water drops varying in size.

Frost—Ice crystal deposits formed by sublimation when temperature/dew point is below freezing.

13. What conditions are necessary for structural icing to occur? (AC 00-6A)

Visible moisture and below-freezing temperatures at the point moisture strikes the aircraft are necessary.

14. Which type of structural icing is more dangerous, rime or clear? (AC 00-6A)

Clear ice is typically the most hazardous ice encountered. It is hard, heavy and tenacious. Clear ice forms when, after initial impact, the remaining liquid portion of the drop flows out over the aircraft surface, gradually freezing as a smooth sheet of solid ice. This happens when drops are large, such as in rain or in cumuliform clouds. Its removal by deicing equipment is especially difficult due to the fact that it forms as it flows away from the deicing equipment.

15. What factors must be present for a thunderstorm to form? (AC 00-6A)

To form a thunderstorm there must be:

a. A source of lift (heating, fast-moving front)

b. Unstable air (nonstandard lapse rate)

c. High moisture content (temperature and dew point are close).

16. What are "squall line" thunderstorms? (AC 00-6A)

A squall line is a non-frontal, narrow band of active thunderstorms. Often it develops ahead of a cold front in moist, unstable air, but it may also develop in unstable air far removed from any front. The line may be too long to easily detour and too wide and severe to penetrate. It often contains severe steady-state thunderstorms and presents the single most intense weather hazard to aircraft. It usually forms rapidly, reaching a maximum intensity during the late afternoon and the first few hours of darkness.

17. State two basic ways that fog may form. (AC 00-6A)

Fog forms:

a. By cooling air to the dew point

b. By adding moisture to the air

18. Name several types of fog. (AC 00-6A)

a. Radiation fog

b. Advection fog

c. Upslope fog

d. Steam fog

e. Precipitation-induced fog

19. What causes radiation fog to form? (AC 00-6A)

Radiation fog is formed when the ground cools the adjacent air to the dew point on calm, clear nights.

20. What is advection fog, and where is it most likely to form? (AC 00-6A)

Advection fog results from the transport of warm, humid air over a cold surface. A pilot can expect advection fog to form primarily along coastal areas during the winter. Unlike radiation fog, it may occur with winds, cloudy skies, over a wide geographic area, and at any time of the day or night.

21. Define upslope fog. (AC 00-6A)

Upslope fog forms when air flows upward over rising terrain and, consequently, is adiabatically cooled to or below its initial dew point. It is commonly found along the western slopes of the Rocky Mountains.

22. Define steam fog. (AC 00-6A)

Steam fog occurs as a result of the movement of cold air over warm water. A good example of this type of fog may be found over and around the Great Lakes area. If the air above is very cold, that air will tend to be unstable, with heating from below causing the air to rise. If the air is considerably unstable (abnormal lapse rate), thunderstorms and turbulence may be expected. If only the lower layers are unstable, a dense low cloud mass, with some icing potential, is most likely.

23. What is precipitation-induced fog? (AC 00-6A)

Precipitation-induced fog is the result of evaporation of rain or drizzle, evaporation occurring while precipitation is falling and/or it has reached the ground. This type of fog is especially associated with warm fronts, although it may occur with or without the presence of fronts.

24. Why is fog a major operational concern to pilots? (AC 00-6A)

Fog is of primary concern during takeoffs and landings because it can reduce vertical and horizontal visibilities to zero-zero. It can occur instantly from a clear condition, making takeoffs, landings, and even taxiing, potentially hazardous operations.

H. Obtaining Weather Information

1. What is the primary means of obtaining a weather briefing? (AIM 7-1-2)

The primary source of preflight weather briefings is an individual briefing obtained from a briefer at the FSS or NWS.

2. What are some examples of other sources of weather information? (AIM 7-1-2)

a. Telephone Information Briefing Service (TIBS) (AFSS)

b. Transcribed Weather Broadcasts (TWEB)

c. Telephone Access to TWEB (TEL-TWEB)

d. Weather and aeronautical information from numerous private industries sources

e. The Direct User Access System (DUATS)

3. What pertinent information should a weather briefing include? (AIM 7-1-3)

a. Adverse conditions

b. VFR flight not recommended

c. Synopsis

d. Current conditions

e. Enroute forecast

f. Destination forecast

g. Winds aloft

h. Notices to Airmen (NOTAMs)

i. ATC delay

In addition, upon request pilots may obtain the following from AFSS/FSS briefers: information on MTRs and MOAs, a review of printed NOTAM publications, approximate density altitude information, information on air traffic services and rules, customs/immigration procedures, ADIZ rules, search and rescue, LORAN-C NOTAMs, GPS RAIM availability, and other assistance as required.

4. What is "EFAS"? (AIM 7-1-4)

Enroute Flight Advisory Service (EFAS) is a service specifically
designed to provide enroute aircraft with timely and meaningful
weather advisories pertinent to the type of flight intended, route of
flight, and altitude. EFAS is also a central collection and distribu-
tion point for pilot-reported weather information (PIREPs). EFAS
provides communications capabilities for aircraft flying at 5,000
feet above ground level to 17,500 feet MSL on a common frequency of 122.0 MHz. It is also known as "Flight Watch." Discrete
EFAS frequencies have been established to ensure communications
coverage from 18,000 through 45,000 feet MSL, serving in each
specific ARTCC area. These discrete frequencies may be used
below 18,000 feet when coverage permits reliable communication.

5. What is "HIWAS"? (AIM 7-1-9)

Hazardous In-flight Weather Advisory Service (HIWAS) is a
continuous broadcast of in-flight weather advisories including
summarized Aviation Weather Warnings, SIGMETs, Convective
SIGMETs, Center Weather Advisories, AIRMETs, and urgent
PIREPs. HIWAS is an additional source of hazardous weather
information which makes this data available on a continuous basis.

I. Aviation Weather Reports and Observations

Aviation Weather Reports

1. What is a METAR? (AC 00-45D)

METAR—Aviation Routine Weather Report, an hourly surface
observation of conditions observed at an airport. This is a new
international weather reporting code now being used by all
countries of the world.

2. Describe the basic elements of a METAR. (AC 00-45D)

A METAR report contains the following sequence of elements:

a. Type of report—two types: METAR (routine observation) and SPECI (special observation)

b. Station designator—ICAO four-letter identifier

c. Time of report—four-digit time group appended with a Z to denote Coordinated Universal Time

d. Wind—five-digit group; first 3 digits is direction of the wind from; next 2 digits is the speed in knots

e. Visibility—reported in statute miles

f. Weather and obstructions to visibility—reported in the format: INTENSITY/PROXIMITY/DESCRIPTOR/PRECIPITATION/ OBSTRUCTION TO VISIBILITY/OTHER

g. Sky conditions—reported in the format: AMOUNT/HEIGHT/ TYPE or VERTICAL VISIBILITY

h. Temperature and dew point—reported in two-digit form in degrees centigrade

i. Altimeter setting—reported in four-digit form in inches of mercury

j. Remarks—operationally significant weather, beginning and ending times of certain weather phenomena and low level wind shear

Example: METAR KBNA 1250Z 33018KT 290V360 1/2SM R31/2700FT +SN BLSNFG VV00800/M03 A2991 RMK RERAE42SNB42

3. Describe several types of Automated Surface Observations now available. (AC 00-45D)

ASOS—Automated Surface Observation System, becoming the primary surface weather observing system of the United States. Installation and operation is a joint effort of the NWS, the FAA and the Department of Defense. ASOS provides continuous minute-by-minute observations and performs the basic functions necessary to generate a Surface Aviation Observation and other weather information. When fully implemented, ASOS will more than double the number of full-time surface weather observing locations (between 900 and 1,700 locations).

AWOS—Automated Weather Observation System, installed by the FAA at selected airports around the country. This system consists of automated reports of ceiling/sky conditions, visibility, temperature, dew point, wind direction/speeds/gusts, altimeter setting, and if certain conditions are met, automated remarks containing density altitude, variable visibility and variable wind direction. Automated observations are broadcast on ground-to-air radio and made available on a telephone answering device.

AMOS—Automatic Meteorological Observing Station is a solid state system capable of automatically observing temperature, dew point, wind direction and speed, pressure (altimeter setting), peak wind speed, and precipitation accumulation. The field sensors are tied directly to the FAA observation network. It transmits a weather report whenever the station is polled by the circuits.

4. What are PIREPs (UA), and where are they usually found? (AC 00-45D)

An abbreviation for "Pilot Reports," they contain information concerning weather as observed by pilots en route. Required elements for all PIREPs are message type, location, time, flight level, type of aircraft, and at least one weather element encountered. All altitudes are MSL unless otherwise noted. Distances are in nautical miles and time is in UTC. A PIREP is usually transmitted as an individual report but can be appended to a surface aviation weather report or placed into collectives.

5. What are Radar Weather Reports (SDs)? (AC 00-45D)

Thunderstorms and general areas of precipitation can be observed by radar. Most radar stations report each hour at H+35, with intervening special reports as required. The report includes the type, intensity, intensity trend and location of the precipitation. Also included is the echo top of the precipitation and if significant, the base echo. All heights are reported above Mean Sea Level (MSL). Radar Weather Reports help pilots plan ahead to avoid thunderstorm areas. Once airborne, however, they must depend on visual sighting or airborne radar to evade individual storms.

J. Aviation Weather Forecasts

1. What are Terminal Aerodrome Forecasts (TAFs)? (AC 00-45D)

A TAF is a concise statement of the expected meteorological conditions at an airport during a specified period (usually 24 hours). TAFs are issued in the following format:

a. Type—2 types: routine forecast issuance and amended forecast issuance

b. Location—ICAO 4-letter location identifiers

c. Issuance time—six-digit group giving date (first 2 digits) and time (last 4 digits) in UTC

d. Valid time—four-digit group giving valid time (usually 24 hours); amended forecasts may be less than 24 hours

e. Forecast—basic format is: WIND/VISIBILITY/WEATHER/ SKY CONDITION

2. What is an Aviation Area Forecast (FA)? (AC 00-45D)

An Aviation Area Forecast (FA) is a forecast of general weather conditions over an area the size of several states. It is used to determine forecast enroute weather and to interpolate conditions at airports which do not have TAFs issued. FAs are issued three times a day for each of the contiguous 48 states.

3. What information is provided by an Aviation Area Forecast (FA)? (AC 00-45D)

The FA is comprised of four sections:

a. Communications and product header section—identifies the office from which the FA is issued, the date and time of issue, the product name, the valid times and the states and/or areas covered by the FA.

b. Precautionary statement section—between the communications/products headers and the body of the forecast are three precautionary statements which are in all Area Forecasts:

> SEE AIRMET SIERRA FOR IFR CONDITIONS
> AND MTN OBSC

Alerts user that IFR conditions and/or mountain obscurement may be occurring or may be forecast to occur in a portion of the FA area.

TSTMS IMPLY PSBL SVR OR GTR TURBC SVR ICG LLWS AND IFR CONDS

A reminder of the hazards existing in all thunderstorms.

NON MSL HGTS ARE DENOTED BY AGL OR CIG

Alerts user that heights, for the most part are above sea level. All heights are in hundreds of feet. The tops of clouds, turbulence, icing and freezing level heights are always MSL. Heights above ground level are noted in either of two ways: ceilings by definition are above ground, therefore, the contraction "CIG" indicates above ground. The contraction "AGL" means above ground level; thus, if the contraction "AGL" or "CIG" is not denoted, height is automatically above MSL.

c. Synopsis section — a brief summary of the location and movements of fronts, pressure systems, and circulation patterns for an 18-hour period. References to low ceilings and/or visibilities, strong winds or any other phenomena the forecaster considers useful may also be included.

d. VFR Clouds and Weather section — This section contains a 12-hour specific forecast, followed by a 6-hour (18-hour in Alaska) categorical outlook giving a total forecast period of 18 hours (30 hours in Alaska). The VFR CLDS/WX section is usually several paragraphs long. The breakdown may be by states or by well-known geographical areas. The specific forecast section gives a general description of clouds and weather which cover an area greater than 3,000 square miles and is significant to VFR flight operations.

4. What are In-flight Aviation Weather Advisories (WST, WS, WA)? (AC 00-45D)

In-flight Aviation Weather Advisories are forecasts to advise enroute aircraft of development of potentially hazardous weather. All heights are referenced to MSL, except in the case of ceilings (CIG) which indicates above ground level. The advisories are of three types: convective SIGMET (WST), SIGMET (WS) and AIRMET (WA).

5. What is a convective SIGMET? (AC 00-45D)

Convective SIGMETs (WST) implies severe or greater turbulence, severe icing and low-level wind shear. They may be issued for any convective situation which the forecaster feels is hazardous to all categories of aircraft. Convective SIGMET bulletins are issued for the Eastern (E), Central (C) and Western (W) United States (convective SIGMETs are not issued for Alaska or Hawaii). Bulletins are issued hourly at H+55. Special bulletins are issued at any time as required and updated at H+55. The text of the bulletin consists of either and observation and a forecast, or just a forecast. The forecast is valid for up to 2 hours.

a. Severe thunderstorm due to:
  i. Surface winds greater than or equal to 50 knots
  ii. Hail at the surface greater than or equal to 3/4 inches in diameter
  iii. Tornadoes
b. Embedded thunderstorms
c. A line of thunderstorms
d. Thunderstorms greater than or equal to VIP level 4 affecting 40 percent or more of an area at least 3,000 square miles.

6. What is a SIGMET (WS)? (AC 00-45D)

A SIGMET (WS) advises of non-convective weather that is potentially hazardous to all aircraft. SIGMETs are issued for the six areas corresponding to the FA areas. The maximum forecast period is four hours. In the conterminous United States, SIGMETs are issued when the following phenomena occur or are expected to occur:

a. Severe icing not associated with a thunderstorm.
b. Severe or extreme turbulence or clear air turbulence (CAT) not associated with thunderstorms.
c. Duststorms, sandstorms or volcanic ash lowering surface or in-flight visibilities to below 3 miles.
d. Volcanic eruption.

7. What is an AIRMET (WA)? (AC 00-45D)

AIRMETs (WA) are advisories of significant weather phenomena but describe conditions at intensities lower than those which trigger SIGMETs. AIRMETs are intended for dissemination to all pilots in the preflight and enroute phase of flight to enhance safety. AIRMET bulletins are issued on a scheduled basis every 6 hours and contain details on one or more of the following phenomena when they occur or are forecast to occur:

a. Moderate icing.

b. Moderate turbulence.

c. Sustained surface winds of 30 knots or more.

d. Ceilings less than 1,000 feet and/or visibilities less than 3 miles. affecting over 50 percent of the area at one time.

e. Extensive mountain obscurement.

8. What is a TWEB? (AC 00-45D)

The Transcribed Weather Enroute Broadcasts (TWEBs) are similar to area forecasts except more specific information is provided in a route format. They provide forecast sky cover height and amount of cloud bases), cloud tops, visibility (including vertical visibility), weather, and obstructions to vision are described for a corridor 25 miles on either side of the route. Cloud bases and tops are always MSL unless noted. Ceilings are always above ground level (AGL). TWEBs are issued by the WSFOs three times per day according to time zone. The TWEB forecast is valid for a 15-hour period.

9. What is a Winds and Temperatures Aloft Forecast (FD)? (AC 00-45D)

Winds and temperatures aloft are forecast for specific locations in the contiguous United States and also for a network of locations in Alaska and Hawaii. Forecasts are made twice daily based on 00Z and 12Z data for use during specific time intervals. FDs contain the following characteristics:

a. A four-digit group will show wind direction, in reference to true north, and wind speed in knots.

Continued

b. A six-digit group will include forecast temperatures in degrees Celsius.

c. Since temperatures above 24,000 feet are always negative, the minus sign is omitted.

d. Through 12,000 feet the levels are true altitude and above 18,000 feet the levels are pressure altitude.

e. No winds are forecast within 1,500 feet of station elevation.

f. No temperatures are forecast for the 3,000-foot level or for any level within 2,500 feet of station elevation.

g. If the coded direction is more than "36," then the wind speed is 100 knots or more.

h. If the wind speed is forecast to be 200 knots or greater, the wind group is coded as 199 knots.

i. When the forecast speed is less than 5 knots, the coded group is "9900" and read "light and variable."

10. What valuable information can be determined from a Winds and Temperatures Aloft Forecast (FD)? (AC 00-45D)

Most favorable altitude—based on winds and direction of flight.

Areas of possible icing—by noting air temperatures of +2°C to -20°C.

Temperature inversions.

Turbulence—by observing abrupt changes in wind direction and speed at different altitudes.

11. What is a Center Weather Advisory (CWA)? (AC 00-45D)

A Center Advisory (CWA) is an unscheduled in-flight air crew, flow control, air traffic advisory for use in anticipating and avoiding adverse weather conditions in the en route and terminal areas. The CWA is not a flight planning forecast but a forecast for conditions beginning within the next two hours. Maximum valid time for a CWA is two hours.

12. What is a Convective Outlook (AC)? (AC 00-45D)

A Convective Outlook (AC) describes the prospects for general thunderstorm activity during the following 24 hours. Areas in which there is high, moderate, or slight risk of severe thunderstorms are included as well as areas where thunderstorms are included as well as areas where thunderstorms may approach severe limits. Outlooks are transmitted at 0700Z and 1500Z and are valid until 1200Z the next day.

K. Aviation Weather Charts

1. Give some examples of current weather charts, which are used in flight planning and available at the FSS or NWSO. (AC 00-45D)

a. Surface Analysis Chart

b. Weather Depiction Chart

c. Radar Summary Chart

d. Significant Weather Prognostic Chart

e. Winds and Temperatures Aloft Chart

f. Composite Moisture Stability Chart

g. Severe Weather Outlook Chart

h. Constant Pressure Analysis Chart

i. Tropopause Data Chart

j. Volcanic Ash Forecast Transport and Dispersion Chart

2. What is a Surface Analysis Chart? (AC 00-45D)

The Surface Analysis Chart is a computer-prepared chart that covers the contiguous 48 states and adjacent areas. The chart is transmitted every three hours. The surface analysis chart provides a ready means of locating pressure systems and fronts. It also gives and overview of winds, temperatures and dew point temperatures at chart time. When using the chart, keep in mind that weather moves and conditions change. Using the surface analysis chart in conjunction with other information gives a more complete weather picture.

3. What information does a Weather Depiction Chart provide? (AC 00-45D)

The Weather Depiction Chart is computer-prepared from Surface
Aviation Observations. This chart gives a broad overview of the
observed flying category conditions at the valid time of the chart.
The chart begins at 01Z each day, is transmitted at three-hour
intervals, and is valid at the time of the plotted data. The plotted
data for each station area are: total sky cover, cloud height or
ceiling, weather and obstructions to vision and visibilities. The
weather depiction chart is an ideal place to begin in preparing for a
weather briefing and flight planning. From this chart one can get a
"bird's eye" view of areas of favorable and adverse weather
conditions at chart time.

4. Define the terms: IFR, MVFR and VFR. (AC 00-45D)

IFR: (Instrument Flight Rules)—Ceilings less than 1,000 feet
and/or visibilities less than 3 miles

MVFR: (Marginal VFR)—Ceiling 1,000 to 3,000 feet inclusive
and/or visibility 3 to 5 miles inclusive

VFR: (Visual Flight Rules)—No ceiling, or ceiling greater than
3,000 feet and visibility greater than 5 miles

5. What are Radar Summary Charts? (AC 00-45D)

A radar summary chart graphically displays a collection of radar
weather reports (SDs). This computer generated chart is con-
structed from regularly scheduled radar observations and is valid at
the time of the reports (H+35), i.e. 35 minutes past each hour.
These charts are available between 16 and 24 hours daily, depending on the system being used. The chart displays the type of
precipitation echoes, their intensity, intensity trend, configuration,
coverage, echo tops and bases, and movement. Severe weather
watches are plotted if they are in effect when the chart is valid. The
radar summary chart aids in preflight planning by identifying
general areas and movement of precipitation and/or thunderstorms.
Anything shown on this chart along or near a pilot's route of flight
must be taken into consideration and noted carefully.

Note: Radar detects only drops or ice particles of precipitation size, it does not detect clouds and fog. Therefore, the absence of echoes does not guarantee clear weather, and cloud tops may be higher than the tops detected by radar. The chart must be used in conjunction with other charts, reports, and forecasts.

6. What are Significant Weather Prognostic charts? (AC 00-45D)

Significant Weather Prognostic charts, called "progs," portray forecast weather that might influence flight planning. Significant weather progs are both manually and computer-prepared for the conterminous United States and adjacent areas. The U.S. low-level significant weather prog is designed for domestic flight planning to 24,000 feet MSL, and a U.S. high-level prog is for domestic flights from 24,000 feet to 63,000 feet MSL. Chart legends include valid time in UTC.

7. Describe a U.S. Low-Level Significant Weather Prog chart. (AC 00-45D)

The low-level prog is a four-panel chart. The two lower panels are 12- and 24-hour surface progs. The two upper panels are 12- and 24-hour progs of significant weather from the surface to 400 millibars (24,000 feet MSL). The charts show conditions as they are forecast to be at the valid time of the chart. This chart is issued four times daily with the 12- and 24-hour forecasts based on the 00Z, 06Z, 12Z and 18Z synoptic data. The two surface prog panels depict fronts, significant troughs and pressure centers and also outlines areas of forecast precipitation and/or thunderstorms. The two upper panels depicts IFR, MVFR, turbulence, and freezing levels.

8. Describe a U.S. High-Level Significant Weather Prog chart. (AC 00-45D)

The U.S. High-Level Significant Weather Prog is derived from forecasts for both domestic and international flights. This prog chart encompasses airspace from 24,000 feet to 63,000 feet pressure altitude over the conterminous United States, Mexico,

Continued

Central America, portions of South America, the western Atlantic and eastern Pacific. The chart is prepared by the U.S. National Meteorological Center and provides users with forecast winds and temperatures aloft along with significant forecast weather.

9. What information may be obtained from the U.S. High-Level Significant Weather Prog charts? (AC 00-45D)

    a. Active thunderstorms

    b. Severe squall lines

    c. Tropical cyclone(s)

    d. From 10,000 feet MSL to FL250 clouds associated with "a" through "c" above

    e. Above FL250, cumulonimbus clouds associated with "a" through "c" above

    f. Moderate or severe turbulence

    g. Moderate or severe icing

    h. Widespread sandstorm/duststorms

    i. Surface positions of well-defined convergence zones

    j. Surface positions, speed and direction of movement of frontal systems

    k. Tropopause height

    l. Jet streams

    m. Volcanic activity

10. What is a Forecast Winds and Temperatures Aloft chart (FD)? (AC 00-45D)

This is a computer-generated chart depicting both observed and forecast winds and temperatures aloft. Forecast winds and temperatures aloft are prepared for eight levels on eight separate panels. The levels are 6,000, 9,000, 12,000, 18,000, 24,000, 30,000, 34,000 and 39,000 feet MSL. They are available daily as 12 hour progs valid at 1200Z and 0000Z. These charts are typically used to determine winds at a proposed altitude or to select the best altitude for a proposed flight. Temperatures also can be determined from the forecast charts. Interpolation must be used to determine winds and temperatures at a level between charts and data when the time period is other than the valid time of the chart.

11. What is a Composite Moisture Stability chart? (AC 00-45D)

The Composite Moisture Stability chart is an analysis chart using observed upper air data. The chart is composed of four panels including stability, freezing level, precipitable water and, average relative humidity. This computer-generated chart is available twice daily with valid times of 12Z and 00Z. The chart is used to determine the characteristics of a particular weather system in terms of stability, moisture, and possible aviation hazards. Even though this chart is several hours old when received, the weather system will tend to move these characteristics with it. Exercise caution, as modification of these characteristics could occur through development, dissipation, or the movement of the system.

12. What is a Severe Weather Outlook chart? (AC 00-45D)

The Severe Weather Outlook chart is a 48-hour outlook for thunderstorm activity. The chart is presented in 2 panels. The left-hand panel covers the first 24-hour period beginning at 12Z and depicts areas of possible general thunderstorm activity as well as severe thunderstorms. The right-hand panel covers the following day beginning at 12Z and is an outlook for the possibility of severe thunderstorms only. This computer-prepared chart is issued once daily in the morning (about 08Z). This chart is strictly for advanced planning. It alerts all interests to the possibility of future thunderstorm development.

13. What are Constant Pressure Analysis charts? (AC 00-45D)

Any surface of equal pressure in the atmosphere is a constant pressure surface. A Constant Pressure Analysis chart is an upper air weather map where all information depicted is at the specified pressure of the chart. From these charts, a pilot can approximate the observed air temperature, wind, and temperature–dew point

Continued

spread along a proposed route. They also depict highs, lows, troughs, and ridges aloft by the height contour patterns resembling isobars on a surface map. Twice daily, six computer prepared constant pressure charts are transmitted by facsimile for six pressure levels:

850 mb	5,000 ft
700 mb	10,000 ft
500 mb	18,000 ft
300 mb	30,000 ft
250 mb	34,000 ft
200 mb	39,000 ft

14. What significance do height "contour" lines have on a Constant Pressure chart? (AC 00-45D)

Heights of the specified pressure for each station are analyzed through the use of solid lines called contours to give a height pattern. The contours depict highs, lows, troughs, and ridges aloft in the same manner as isobars on the surface chart. Also, closely-spaced contours mean strong winds, as do closely-spaced isobars.

15. What significance do "isotherms" have on a Constant Pressure chart? (AC 00-45D)

Isotherms (dashed lines) drawn at 5°C-intervals show horizontal temperature variations at chart altitude. By inspecting isotherms, you can determine if your flight will be toward colder or warmer air. Subfreezing temperatures and a temperature/dewpoint spread of 5°C or less suggest possible icing.

16. What significance do the "isotach" lines have on a Constant Pressure chart? (AC 00-45D)

Isotachs are lines of equal or constant wind speed and appear only on the 300 and 200 mb charts. Isotachs are drawn at 20-knot intervals beginning with 10 knots. To aid in identifying areas of strong winds, hatching denotes wind speeds of 70 to 110 knots, a clear area within a hatched area indicates 110 to 150 knots, an area of 150 to 190 knots of wind is hatched, etc.

17. Describe a Tropopause Data chart. (AC 00-45D)

The Tropopause Data chart is a two-panel chart containing a maximum wind prog and a vertical wind shear prog. The chart is prepared for the contiguous 48 states and is available once a day with a valid time of 18Z. Both panels show forecast parameters at the tropopause level. The first panel depicts the forecast winds at the tropopause and the second panel gives the tropopause height and vertical wind shear. The panels may be used to determine vertical and horizontal wind shear as clues to probable wind shear turbulence. The charts may also be used to determine winds for high level flight planning.

18. Describe a Volcanic Ash Forecast Transport and Dispersion chart. (AC 00-45D)

This VAFTAD product presents the relative concentrations of ash following a volcanic eruption for three layers of the atmosphere in addition to a composite of ash concentration through the atmosphere. The chart focuses on hazards to aircraft flight operations caused by volcanic eruption with an emphasis on the ash cloud location in time and space. It uses National Meteorological Center forecast data to determine the location of ash concentrations over 6-hour and 12-hour time intervals. The chart is strictly for advanced flight planning purposes, and it is not intended to take the place of SIGMETs regarding volcanic eruptions and ash.

Departure 2

A. Authority and Limitations of the Pilot

1. Discuss 14 CFR 91.3, "Responsibility and Authority of PIC." (14 CFR 91.3)

The pilot-in-command of an aircraft is directly responsible for, and is the final authority as to the operation of that aircraft.

2. What are the right-of-way rules pertaining to IFR flights? (14 CFR 91.113)

When weather conditions permit, regardless of whether an operation is under IFR or VFR, vigilance shall be maintained by each person operating an aircraft so as to see and avoid other aircraft.

3. What are the required reports for equipment malfunction under IFR in controlled airspace? (AIM 5-3-3)

You must report:

a. Loss of VOR, TACAN, ADF, or low-frequency navigation receiver capability.

b. Complete or partial loss of ILS receiver capability.

c. Impairment of air/ground communication capability.

d. Loss of any other equipment installed in the aircraft which may impair safety and/or the ability to operate under IFR.

B. Departure Clearance

1. How can your IFR clearance be obtained? (AIM 5-1-7)

a. At airports with an ATC tower in operation, clearances may be received from either ground control or a specific clearance delivery frequency when available.

b. At airports without a tower or FSS on the field, or in an outlying area:
   i. Clearances may be received over the radio through a RCO (remote communication outlet) or, in some cases, over the telephone.

Continued

    ii. In some areas, a clearance delivery frequency is available that is usable at different airports within a particular geographic area, for example, Class B airspace.

    iii. If the above methods are not available, your clearance can be obtained from ARTCC once you are airborne, provided you remain VFR in Class E airspace.

The procedure may vary due to geographical features, weather conditions, and the complexity of the ATC system. To determine the most effective means of receiving an IFR clearance, pilots should ask the nearest FSS the most appropriate means of obtaining their IFR clearance.

2. What does "cleared as filed" mean? (AIM 5-2-3)

ATC will issue an abbreviated IFR clearance based on the route of flight as filed in the IFR flight plan, provided the filed route can be approved with little or no revision.

3. Which clearance items are given in an abbreviated IFR clearance? (AIM 5-2-3)

C learance Limit (destination airport or fix)
R oute (initial heading)
A ltitude (initial altitude)
F requency (departure)
T ransponder (squawk code)

4. What does "clearance void time" mean? (AIM 5-2-4)

When operating from an airport without a tower, a pilot may receive a clearance containing a provision that if the flight has not departed by a specific time, the clearance is void.

A pilot who does not depart prior to the clearance void time must advise ATC as soon as possible of his/her intentions. ATC will normally notify the pilot of the time allotted to notify ATC. This time cannot exceed 30 minutes.

5. What is the purpose of the term "hold for release" when included in an IFR clearance? (AIM 5-2-4)

ATC may issue "hold for release" instructions in a clearance to delay an aircraft's departure for traffic management reasons (weather, traffic volume, etc.). A pilot may not depart utilizing that IFR clearance until a release time or additional instructions are received from ATC.

C. Departure Procedures

1. What is a SID? (AIM 5-2-6)

A SID (Standard Instrument Departure) is an ATC-coded departure procedure established at certain airports to simplify clearance delivery procedures. They provide a transition procedure from the terminal to the enroute structure. SIDs are in two basic forms: pilot navigation SIDs and vector SIDs. All effective SIDs are published in textual and graphic form in the Terminal Procedures Publication (TPP) by the NOS.

2. Must you accept a SID if assigned one? (AIM 5-2-6)

No, you are not required to accept a SID. If you do not possess a textual description or graphic depiction of the SID you cannot accept one. Also, if for any other reason you cannot accept the SID, you must advise ATC. ATC prefers you let them know ahead of time in the Remarks section of your flight plan.

3. What minimums are necessary for IFR takeoff under 14 CFR Part 91? Under 14 CFR Parts 121, 129, and 135? (14 CFR 91.175)

Except when nonstandard takeoff minimums apply as noted on the approach chart, none for 14 CFR Part 91.

Under 14 CFR 121, 129 and 135:

For 2 engines or less .... 1 SM visibility
For more than 2 engines .... $^1/_2$ SM visibility

4. How does a pilot determine if nonstandard takeoff minimums exist at a particular airport? (AIM 5-2-6)

A large "T" in a black triangle at the bottom of the approach chart of the departure airport indicates that nonstandard takeoff minimums and/or departures procedures exist.

5. What is considered "good operating practice" in determining takeoff minimums for IFR flight?

If an instrument approach procedure has been prescribed for that airport, use the minimums for that approach for takeoff. If no approach procedure is available, basic VFR minimums would be recommended (1,000 feet and 3 miles).

6. Where can a pilot find nonstandard takeoff minimums if they apply? (AIM 5-2-6)

Airports with takeoff minimums other than standard (one statute mile for aircraft having two engines or less and one-half statute mile for aircraft having more than two engines) are described in separate listings on separate pages titled "IFR Takeoff Minimums and Departure Procedures," at the front of each U.S. Government Terminal Procedures Publications (TPP).

7. What is the standard minimum climb gradient for all standard instrument departures? (AIM 5-2-6)

200 feet per nautical mile is the standard climb gradient.

8. When a SID specifies a climb gradient in excess of 200 feet per nautical mile, what significance should this have to the pilot? (AIM 5-2-6)

Climb gradients are specified when required for obstacle clearance. Crossing restrictions in the SIDs may be established for traffic separation or obstacle clearance. When no gradient is specified, the pilot is expected to climb at least 200 feet per nautical mile to the MEA, unless required to level off by a crossing restriction.

9. A climb gradient of 300 feet per nautical mile at a groundspeed of 100 knots requires what rate of climb? (Instrument Approach Procedures SID Chart)

Ground speed divided by 60 seconds times climb gradient = feet per minute; therefore:

$$\frac{100}{60} \ \text{x} \ \ 300 \ = \ 498 \ \text{feet per minute}$$

10. What is the recommended procedure concerning climb rate, when issued a climb to an assigned altitude by ATC? (AIM 4-4-9)

When ATC has not used the term "At Pilot's Discretion" nor imposed any climb or descent restrictions, pilots should initiate climb or descent promptly upon acknowledgment. Descend or climb at an optimum rate consistent with the operating characteristics of the aircraft to 1,000 feet above or below the assigned altitude, then attempt to descent or climb at a rate of between 500 and 1,500 feet per minute until the assigned altitude is reached.

D. VOR Accuracy Checks

1. What are the different methods for checking the accuracy of VOR equipment? (14 CFR 91.171)

a. A VOR Test Signal (VOT) check; ±4°

b. A ground checkpoint; ±4°

c. An airborne checkpoint; ±6°

d. A dual VOR check; within 4° of each other

e. Select a radial over a known ground point; ±6°

A repair station can use a radiated test signal, but only the technician performing the test can make an entry in the logbook.

2. What records must be kept concerning VOR checks? (14 CFR 91.171)

Each person making a VOR check shall enter the date, place and bearing error, and sign the aircraft log or other reliable record.

3. Where can a pilot find the location of airborne check points, ground check points and VOT testing stations? (AIM 1-1-4)

Locations of airborne checkpoints, ground checkpoints, and VOTs are published in the A/FD. They are also depicted on the A/G voice communication panels of the NOS IFR area chart, and IFR enroute low-altitude chart.

E. Transponder

1. Where is altitude encoding transponder equipment required? (AIM 4-1-19)

In general, the regulations require aircraft to be equipped with Mode C transponders when operating:

a. At or above 10,000 feet MSL over the 48 contiguous states or the District of Columbia, excluding that airspace below 2,500 feet AGL;

b. Within 30 miles of a Class B airspace primary airport, below 10,000 feet MSL;

c. Within and above all Class C airspace, up to 10,000 feet MSL;

d. Within 10 miles of certain designated airports, excluding that airspace which is both outside the Class D surface area and below 1,200 feet AGL;

e. All aircraft flying into, within, or across the contiguous United States ADIZ.

2. What are the following transponder codes?
(AIM 6-2-2, 6-3-4 and 6-4-2)

1200	VFR
7700	Emergency
7600	Communications Emergency
7500	Hijacking in progress

3. **Discuss transponder operation in the event of a two-way communications failure.** (AIM 6-4-2)

If an aircraft with a coded radar beacon transponder experiences a loss of two-way radio capability, the pilot should adjust the transponder to reply on Mode A/3, Code 7600. *Note:* The pilot should understand that the aircraft might not be in an area of radar coverage.

F. Airport Facilities

1. **Where can a pilot find information concerning facilities available for a particular airport?** (AIM 9-1-4)

In the Airport/Facility Directory; it contains information concerning services available, communication data, navigational facilities, special notices, etc. The A/FD is reissued in its entirety every 56 days.

2. **What do the following acronyms and abbreviations stand for?** (AIM 2-1-1, 2-1-2 and 2-1-3)

ALS ....Approach Light System
VASI..Visual Approach Slope Indicator
PAPI ....Precision Approach Path Indicator
REIL ....Runway End Identifier Lights

3. **What color are runway edge lights?** (AIM 2-1-4)

The runway edge lights are white—except on instrument runways, yellow replaces white on the last 2,000 feet or half the runway length, whichever is less, to form a caution zone for landings.

4. **What colors and color combinations are standard airport rotating beacons?** (AIM 2-1-8)

Lighted Land Airport ....White/Green
Lighted Water Airport ....White/Yellow
Military Airport ....2 White/Green

5. **What does the operation of a rotating beacon at an airport within Class D airspace during daylight hours mean?** (AIM 2-1-8)

In Class B, Class C, Class D, and Class E surface areas, operation of the airport beacon during the hours of daylight often indicates that the ground visibility is less than 3 miles and/or the ceiling is less than 1,000 feet. ATC clearance in accordance with 14 CFR Part 91 is required for landing, takeoff and flight in the traffic pattern. Pilots should not rely solely on the operation of the airport beacon to indicate if weather conditions are IFR or VFR. There is no regulatory requirement for daylight operation and it is the pilot's responsibility to comply with proper preflight planning as required by 14 CFR Part 91.

6. **Where would information concerning runway lengths, widths and weight bearing capacities be found?** (A/FD)

The Airport/Facility Directory has this information.

7. **What are runway touchdown zone markings?** (AIM 2-3-3)

Touchdown zone markings identify the touchdown zone for landing operations and are coded to provide distance information in 500-foot increments. These markings consist of groups of one, two, and three rectangular bars symmetrically arranged in pairs about the runway centerline. Normally, the standard glide slope angle of 3 degrees, if flown to the surface, will ensure touchdown within this zone.

8. **What is the purpose of runway aiming point markings?** (AIM 2-3-3)

The aiming point markings serve as a visual aiming point for a landing aircraft. These two rectangular markings consist of a broad white stripe, located on each side of the runway centerline, and approximately 1,000 feet from the landing threshold. The pilot can estimate a visual glide path that will intersect the marking ensuring a landing within the 3,000-foot touchdown zone.

9. How far down a runway does the touchdown zone extend? (Pilot/Controller Glossary)

The touchdown zone is the first 3,000 feet of the runway beginning at the threshold. The area is used for determination of Touchdown Zone Elevation in the development of straight-in landing minimums for instrument approaches.

En Route   **3**

A. Enroute Limitations

1. Define the following. (Pilot/Controller Glossary)

MEA—Minimum Enroute Altitude; the lowest published altitude between radio fixes which ensures acceptable navigational signal coverage and meets obstacle clearance requirements.

MOCA—Minimum Obstacle Clearance Altitude; the lowest published altitude between radio fixes that meets obstacle clearance requirements. It also ensures acceptable navigational signal coverage within 22 NM of VOR.

MCA—Minimum Crossing Altitude; the lowest altitude at certain fixes at which aircraft must cross when proceeding in the direction of a higher MEA.

MRA—Minimum Reception Altitude; the lowest altitude at which an intersection can be determined.

MAA—Maximum Authorized Altitude; the maximum altitude usable for a route segment that ensures signal reception without interference from another signal on the same frequency.

MORCA—Minimum Off-Route Obstruction Clearance Altitude; this provides obstruction clearance with a 1,000-foot buffer in non-mountainous terrain areas and a 2,000-foot buffer in designated mountainous areas within the United States. This altitude might not provide signal coverage from ground-based navigational aids, Air Traffic Control radar, or communications coverage.

2. If no applicable minimum altitude is prescribed (no MEA or MOCA), what minimum altitudes apply for IFR operations? (14 CFR 91.177)

Minimum altitudes are:

a. Mountainous terrain—at least 2,000 feet above the highest obstacle within a horizontal distance of 4 NM from the course to be flown.

b. Other than mountainous terrain—at least 1,000 feet above the highest obstacle within a horizontal distance of 4 NM from the course to be flown.

3. **What cruising altitudes shall be maintained while operating under IFR in controlled airspace (Class A, B, C, D, or E)? In uncontrolled airspace (Class G)?** (14 CFR 91.179)

IFR flights within controlled airspace (Class A, B, C, D, or E) shall maintain the altitude or flight level assigned by ATC. In uncontrolled airspace (Class G), altitude is selected based on the magnetic course flown:

Below 18,000 feet MSL:
   0 to 179° .... odd thousand MSL
   180 to 359° .... even thousand MSL

18,000 feet up to but not including 29,000 feet MSL:
   0 to 179° .... odd flight levels
   180 to 359° .... even flight levels

4. **What procedures are applicable concerning courses to be flown when operating IFR?** (14 CFR 91.181)

Except when maneuvering an aircraft to pass well clear of other air traffic, or the maneuvering of an aircraft in VFR conditions to clear the intended flight path (both before and during climb and descent), the following applies:

a. Maintain the centerline of a federal airway

b. Maintain a direct route between navigational aids or fixes defining the route.

5. **Where are the compulsory reporting points, if any, on a direct flight not flown on radials, or courses of established airways or routes?** (AIM 5-3-2)

They are reporting points that must be reported to ATC. They are designated on aeronautical charts by solid triangles, or filed in a flight plan as fixes selected to define direct routes.

B. Enroute Procedures

1. What reports should be made to ATC at all times without a specific request? (AIM 5-3-3)

The pilot must report:

a. When vacating any previously assigned altitude or flight level for a newly assigned altitude or flight level.

b. When an altitude change will be made if operating on a clearance specifying VFR-On-Top.

c. When unable to climb/descend at a rate of at least 500 feet per minute.

d. When approach has been missed (request clearance for specific action; i.e., to alternate airport, another approach, etc.).

e. Change in the average true speed (at cruising altitude) when it varies by 5 percent or 10 knots (whichever is greater) from that filed in the flight plan.

f. The time and altitude or flight level upon reaching a holding fix or point that the pilot is cleared to.

g. When leaving any assigned holding fix or point.

h. Any loss, in controlled airspace, of VOR, TACAN, ADF, low frequency navigation receiver capability, complete or partial loss of ILS receiver capability or impairment of air/ground communications capability.

i. Any information relating to the safety of flight.

j. Upon encountering weather or hazardous conditions not forecast.

2. What reporting requirements are required by ATC when not in radar contact? (AIM 5-3-3)

a. When leaving final approach fix inbound on the final (nonprecision) approach, or when leaving the outer marker (or fix used in lieu of the outer marker) inbound on final (precision) approach.

b. A corrected estimate at anytime it becomes apparent that an estimate as previously submitted is in error in excess of 3 minutes.

3. What items of information should be included in every position report? (AIM 5-3-2)

a. Identification

b. Position

c. Time

d. Altitude or flight level

e. Type of flight plan (not required in IFR position reports made directly to ARTCCs or approach control)

f. ETA and name of next reporting point

g. The name only of the next succeeding reporting point along the route of flight, and

h. Pertinent remarks

4. Are you required to report unforecast weather encountered en route? (AIM 5-3-3)

Yes; pilots encountering weather conditions which have not been forecast, or hazardous conditions which have been forecast, are expected to forward a report of such weather to ATC.

5. Explain the terms "maintain" and "cruise" as they pertain to an IFR altitude assignment. (AIM 4-4-3)

Maintain—Self-explanatory: maintain last altitude assigned.

Cruise—Used instead of "maintain" to assign a block of airspace to a pilot, from minimum IFR altitude up to and including the altitude specified in the cruise clearance. The pilot may level off at any intermediate altitude, and climb/descent may be made at the discretion of the pilot. However, once the pilot starts a descent, and *verbally* reports leaving an altitude in the block, he may not return to that altitude without additional ATC clearance.

6. When will ATC issue a "cruise clearance"?

ATC will usually issue a cruise clearance when:

a. Conditions permit a pilot to proceed to, descend, make an approach and land at an airport that is either within/below/outside controlled airspace and without a standard instrument approach procedure.

b. Conditions such as bad weather or turbulence call for more flexibility for the pilot to avoid weather turbulence.

A cruise clearance can be used in conjunction with an airport clearance limit when it is to allow the pilot the capability to proceed to the destination airport, descend and land in accordance with applicable regulations.

7. Why would a pilot request a VFR-On-Top clearance? (AIM 4-4-7)

A pilot on an IFR flight plan operating in VFR weather conditions, may request VFR-On-Top in lieu of an assigned altitude. For reasons such as turbulence, more favorable winds aloft, etc., the pilot has the flexibility to select an altitude or flight level of his/her choice (subject to any ATC restrictions). Pilots desiring to climb through a cloud, haze, smoke, or other meteorological formation and then either cancel their IFR flight plan or operate VFR-On-Top may request a climb to VFR-On-Top.

8. Is a VFR-On-Top clearance a VFR clearance or an IFR clearance? (AIM 4-4-7)

A VFR-On-Top clearance is an IFR clearance.

9. Which airspace prohibits VFR-On-Top clearances? (AIM 4-4-7)

Class A airspace.

10. What operational procedures must pilots on IFR flight plans adhere to when operating VFR-On-Top? (AIM 4-4-7)

They must:

a. Fly at the appropriate VFR altitude

b. Comply with the VFR visibility and distance from cloud criteria

c. Comply with instrument flight rules that are applicable to this flight; i.e., minimum IFR altitudes, position reporting, radio communications, course to be flown, adherence to ATC clearance, etc.

11. What is a "clearance limit" and when is it received? (AIM 4-4-3)

A traffic clearance issued prior to departure will normally authorize flight to the airport of intended landing. Under certain conditions, at some locations, a short-range clearance procedure is used, whereby a clearance is issued to a fix within or just outside of the terminal area, and pilots are advised of the frequency on which they will receive the long-range clearance direct from the center controller.

12. What information will ATC provide when they request a hold at a fix where the holding pattern is not charted? (AIM 5-3-7)

An ATC clearance requiring an aircraft to hold at a fix where the pattern is not charted will include the following information:

a. Direction of holding from the fix, in reference to the eight cardinal compass points (i.e. N, NE, E, SE, etc.).

b. Holding fix (the fix may be omitted if included at the beginning of the transmission as the clearance limit).

c. Radial, course, bearing, airway or route on which the aircraft is to hold.

d. Leg length in miles if DME or RNAV is to be used (leg length will be specified in minutes on pilot request or if the controller considers it necessary).

e. Direction of turns, if holding pattern is nonstandard (left turns), the pilot requests direction of turns, or the controller considers it necessary to state direction of turns.

f. Time to expect further clearance and any pertinent additional delay information.

13. What are the maximum airspeeds permitted for aircraft while holding? (AIM 5-3-7)

MHA – 6,000 ft .... 200 KIAS
6,001 – 14,000 ft .... 230 KIAS
14,001 – and above .... 265 KIAS

Note: Holding patterns at all altitudes may be restricted to a maximum speed of 175 KIAS. Holding patterns from 6,001 to 14,000 feet may be restricted to a maximum airspeed of 210 KIAS. These nonstandard patterns will be depicted by an icon.

14. What is a nonstandard versus a standard holding pattern? (AIM 5-3-7)

In a standard pattern, all turns are to the right. In a nonstandard pattern, all turns are to the left.

15. Describe the procedure for crosswind correction in a holding pattern. (AIM 5-3-7)

Compensate for wind effect primarily by drift correction on the inbound and outbound legs. When outbound, triple the inbound drift correction to avoid major turning adjustments.

16. What action is appropriate when approaching a holding fix at an airspeed in excess of maximum holding speed? (AIM 5-3-7)

Start a speed reduction when 3 minutes or less from the fix. Speed may be reduced earlier, but ATC must be advised of the change.

17. Why is it important for the pilot to receive an EFC time with initial holding instructions? (AIM 5-3-7)

In case of lost communications, the pilot will know when to depart the holding pattern.

18. Describe the different recommended entry methods for holding. (AIM 5-3-7)

The three types of entry are:

a. Parallel

b. Teardrop

c. Direct

19. What is the leg length for a standard holding pattern? (AIM 5-3-7)

The standard leg length is:

a. 1 minute inbound at or below 14,000 feet MSL, and

b. $1^1/_2$ minutes inbound above 14,000 feet MSL.

20. If assigned a DME hold, what procedures should be utilized? (AIM 5-3-7)

The same entry and holding procedures apply to DME holding, except distances (nautical miles) are used instead of time values. The outbound course of the DME holding pattern is called the outbound leg of the pattern. The length of the outbound leg will be specified by the controller, and the end of this leg is determined by the DME readout.

C. Oxygen Requirements

1. What regulations apply concerning supplemental oxygen? (14 CFR 91.211)

a. At cabin pressure altitudes above 12,500 MSL up to and including 14,000 MSL, the minimum flight crew must use oxygen after 30 minutes.

b. Above 14,000 MSL up to and including 15,000 MSL, the minimum flight crew must continuously use oxygen.

c. Above 15,000 MSL, each passenger must be provided with supplemental oxygen and the minimum flight crew must continuously use oxygen.

D. Emergencies

1. When may the pilot-in-command of an aircraft deviate from an ATC clearance? (14 CFR 91.123)

Except in an emergency, no person may, in an area in which air traffic control is exercised, operate an aircraft contrary to an ATC instruction.

2. If an emergency action requires deviation from 14 CFR Part 91, must a pilot submit a written report, and if so, to whom? (14 CFR 91.123)

Each pilot-in-command who is given priority by ATC in an emergency shall, if requested by ATC, submit a detailed report of that emergency within 48 hours to the chief of that ATC facility.

3. Concerning two-way radio communications failure in VFR and IFR conditions, what is the procedure for altitude, route, leaving holding fix, descent for approach, and approach selection? (14 CFR 91.185)

In VFR conditions: If the failure occurs in VFR, or if VFR is encountered after the failure, each pilot shall continue the flight under VFR and land as soon as practicable.

Continued

In IFR conditions: If the failure occurs in IFR conditions, or if VFR conditions are not within range, each pilot shall continue the flight according to the following:

a. Route:

   i. By the route assigned in the last ATC clearance received;

   ii. If being radar-vectored, by the direct route from the point of radio failure to the fix, route, or airway specified in the vector clearance;

   iii. In the absence of an assigned route, a route that ATC has advised may be expected in a further clearance; or

   iv. In the absence of an assigned route or a route that ATC has advised may be expected in a further clearance, by the route filed in the flight plan.

b. Altitude: At the highest of the following altitudes or flight levels for the route segment being flown:

   i. The altitude or flight level assigned in the last ATC clearance received;

   ii. The minimum altitude (converted, if appropriate, to minimum flight level) for IFR operations; or

   iii. The altitude or flight level ATC has advised may be expected in a further clearance.

c. Leave clearance limit:

   i. When the clearance limit is a fix from which the approach begins, commence descent or descent and approach as close as possible to the expect-further-clearance time if one has been received; or if one has not been received, as close as possible to the estimated time of arrival as calculated from the filed or amended (with ATC) estimated time en route.

   ii. If the clearance limit is not a fix from which the approach begins, leave the clearance limit at the expect-further-clearance time if one has been received; or if none has been received, upon arrival over the clearance limit, and proceed to a fix from which an approach begins and commence descent or decent and approach as close as possible to the estimated time of arrival as calculated from the filed or amended (with ATC) estimated time en route.

4. Assuming two-way communications failure, discuss the recommended procedure to follow concerning altitudes to be flown for the following trip:

The MEA between A and B is 5,000 feet; the MEA between B and C is 5,000 feet; the MEA between C and D is 11,000 feet; and the MEA between D and E is 7,000 feet. You have been cleared via A, B, C, D, to E. While flying between A and B, your assigned altitude was 6,000 feet and you were told to expect a clearance to 8,000 feet at B. Prior to receiving the higher altitude assignment, you experience two-way communication failure. (AIM 6-4-1)

The correct procedure would be as follows:

a. Maintain 6,000 feet to B, then climb to 8,000 feet (the altitude you were advised to expect).

b. Continue to maintain 8,000 feet, then climb to 11,000 feet at C, or prior to C if necessary to comply with an MCA at C.

c. Upon reaching D, you would descend to 8,000 feet (even though the MEA was 7,000 feet), as 8,000 feet was the highest of the altitude situations stated in the rule.

5. What procedure would you use if all communication and navigation equipment failed (complete electrical system failure)?

a. First, determine you have complete loss. Determine the cause (check circuit breakers, alternator, ammeter, etc.).

b. Review the preflight weather briefing for the nearest VFR; determine heading and altitude and proceed to VFR conditions, using VFR altitudes.

c. If VFR conditions are not within range of the aircraft, get off the airway and determine the heading to an unpopulated area relatively free of obstructions (terrain or man-made; i.e. rural areas, large lakes, ocean, etc.).

d. Establish a descent on a specific heading to VFR conditions; proceed VFR to the nearest airport.

E. Radio Orientation

1. What angular deviation from a VOR course is represented by half-scale deflection of the CDI? (AC 61-27C, Ch. 8)

Full scale deflection = $10°$; therefore, half-scale deflection = $5°$

2. What distance off-course would an aircraft be with half-scale deflection 30 miles out? (AC 61-27C, Ch. 8)

Aircraft displacement from course is approximately 200 feet per dot per mile.

Example:

$$\frac{200 \times (2.5 \times 30)}{6,000} = \frac{15,000}{6,000} = 2.5 \text{ NM off}$$

Remember: 1 dot 30 miles out = 1 NM off
1 dot 60 miles out = 2 NM off

3. How do you determine time and distance from a VOR station? (AC 61-27C, Ch. 8)

a. Determine the radial on which you are located.

b. Turn 80° right, or left, of the inbound course, rotating the OBS to the nearest 10° increment opposite the direction of turn.

c. Maintain heading. When the CDI centers, note the time.

d. Maintaining the same heading, rotate the OBS 10° in the same direction as above.

e. Note the elapsed time when the CDI again centers.

f. Time/distance from the station is determined by the following formulas:

Time to station:

$$\frac{\text{Time in seconds between bearing change}}{\text{degrees in bearing change}}$$

Distance to station:

$$\frac{\text{TAS x minutes flown}}{\text{degrees of bearing change}}$$

Note: This same formula may be used for ADF.

4. What degree of accuracy can be expected in VOR navigation? (AC 61-27C, Ch. 8)

VOR navigation is accurate to ±1°.

5. How do you find an ADF relative bearing? (AC 61-27C, Ch. 8)

A relative bearing is the angular relationship between the aircraft heading and the station, measured clockwise from the nose. The bearing is read directly on the ADF dial, measured clockwise from zero.

6. How do you find an ADF magnetic bearing? (AC 61-27C, Ch. 8)

A magnetic bearing is the direction of an imaginary line from the aircraft to the station or the station to the aircraft referenced to magnetic north. To determine, use this formula:

MH + RB = MB
(Magnetic heading + relative bearing = magnetic bearing)

If the sum is more than 360, subtract 360 to get the magnetic bearing to the station. The reciprocal of this number is the magnetic bearing from the station.

7. What is ADF homing? (AC 61-27C, Ch. 8)

ADF homing is flying the aircraft on any heading required to keep the ADF needle on zero until the station is reached.

8. What is ADF tracking? (AC 61-27C, Ch. 8)

ADF tracking is a procedure used to fly a straight geographic flight path inbound to or from an NDB. A heading is established that will maintain the desired track, compensating for wind drift.

9. When tracking inbound to an NDB with a 10 degree right wind drift correction angle, what will the relative bearing to the station be? (AC 61-27C, Ch. 8)

350 degrees.

F. Attitude Instrument Flying

1. What are the three fundamental skills involved in attitude instrument flying? (AC 61-27C, Ch. 5)

The three fundamentals are:

a. Instrument cross check (scan)

b. Instrument interpretation

c. Aircraft control

2. Attitude instrument flying involves grouping instruments as they relate to control function as well as aircraft performance. What are the three major groups and what instruments are in each? (AC 61-27C, Ch. 5)

PITCH	BANK	POWER
Attitude Indicator	Attitude Indicator	Manifold Pressure Gauge
Altimeter	Directional Gyro	Tachometer
Airspeed	Turn Coordinator	Airspeed
Vertical Speed		

3. Define what "primary" and "supporting" instruments are, as they pertain to basic attitude instrument flying. (AC 61-27C, Ch. 5)

For any maneuver or condition of flight, the pitch, bank, and power control requirements are most clearly indicated by certain key instruments. Those instruments which provide the most pertinent and essential information are referred to as the "primary" instruments. "Supporting" instruments back up and supplement the information shown on the primary instruments.

4. **What instruments are primary for pitch, bank, and power in straight and level flight?** (AC 61-27C, Ch. 5)

The altimeter is primary for pitch, the directional gyro is primary for bank, and the airspeed indicator is primary for power in level flight.

5. **Describe the procedure for leveling off from a descent at descent airspeed, and for a speed higher than descent airspeed.** (AC 61-27C, Ch. 5)

Low-airspeed level off: begin level off 50 feet above the target altitude.

High-airspeed level off: begin adding power 150 feet above the target altitude. Begin level off 50 feet above target altitude.

G. Unusual Flight Conditions

1. **If a thunderstorm is inadvertently encountered, what flight instrument and what procedure should be used to maintain control of the aircraft?** (AC 00-6A, Ch. 11)

Attitude Indicator—establish power for the recommended maneuvering speed and attempt to maintain a constant *attitude* only. Do not attempt to maintain a constant *altitude*.

2. **What are the conditions needed for major structural icing to form?** (AC 00-6A, Ch. 10)

Structural ice requires:

a. Visible moisture

b. Air temperature near or below freezing

c. Freezing aircraft surface

3. **What action is recommended if you inadvertently encounter icing conditions?** (AC 00-6A, Ch. 10)

    a. Change course and/or altitude

    b. Usually, climb to a higher altitude

4. **Which type of precipitation will produce the most hazardous icing conditions?** (AC 00-6A, Ch. 10)

Freezing rain produces the most hazardous icing conditions.

5. **If icing is inadvertently encountered, how would your landing approach procedure be different?** (AC 00-6A, Ch. 10)

The following guidelines may be used when flying an airplane which has accumulated ice:

    a. Maintain more power during the approach.

    b. Maintain a higher airspeed.

    c. Expect a higher stall speed.

    d. Expect a longer landing roll.

    e. A "no flaps" approach is recommended.

    f. Maintain a consistently higher altitude than normal.

    g. Avoid a missed approach (get it right the first time).

H. Radio Navigation

1. **Within what frequency range do VORs operate?** (AIM 1-1-3)

VORs operate within the 108.0 to 117.95 MHz VHF band.

2. **What are the normal usable distances for the various classes of VOR stations?** (AC 61-27C, Ch. 7)

H-VORs and L-VORs have a normal usable distance of 40 nautical miles below 18,000 feet. T-VORs are short-range facilities which have a power output of approximately 50 watts and a usable distance of 25 nautical miles at 12,000 feet and below. T-VORs are used primarily for instrument approaches in terminal areas, on or adjacent to airports.

Terminal = 1,000 to 12,000 AGL .... 25 NM

Low-altitude = 1,000 to 18,000 AGL .... 40 NM

High-altitude = 1,000 to 14,500 AGL .... 40 NM

High-altitude = 14,500 to 18,000 AGL .... 100 NM

High-altitude = 18,000 to 45,000 AGL .... 130 NM

High-altitude = 45,000 to 60,000 AGL .... 100 NM

3. What is the meaning of a single coded identification received only once every 30 seconds from a VORTAC station? (AIM 1-1-7 and 1-1-13)

The DME component is operative; the VOR component is inoperative. It is important to recognize which identifier is retained for the operative facility. A single coded identifier with a repeat interval every 30 seconds indicates DME is operative. If no identification is received, the facility has been taken off the air for tune-up or repair, even though intermittent or constant signals are received.

4. Will all VOR stations have capability for providing distance information to aircraft equipped with DME? (AIM 1-1-7)

No, aircraft receiving equipment ensures reception of azimuth and distance information from a common source only when designated as VOR/DME, VORTAC, ILS/DME, and LOC/DME stations.

5. For operations off established airways at 17,000 feet MSL, H-Class VORTAC facilities used to define a direct route of flight should be no farther than what distance from each other? (AIM 5-1-7)

They should be no farther than 200 NM apart.

6. **Within what frequency range do NDBs normally operate?** (AIM 1-1-2)

   NDBs operate within the low- to medium-frequency band—190 to 535 kHz.

7. **When a radio beacon is used in conjunction with an ILS marker beacon, what is it called?** (AIM 1-1-2)

   It is called a compass locator.

8. **There are four types of NDB facilities in use. What are they and what are their effective ranges?** (AC 61-27C, Ch. 8)

   HH facilities: 2,000 watts .... 75 NM
   H facilities: 50 to 1,999 watts .... 50 NM
   MH facilities: less than 50 watts .... 25 NM
   ILS compass locator: less than 25 watts .... 15 NM

9. **What limitations apply when using an NDB for navigation?** (AIM 1-1-2)

   Radio beacons are subject to disturbances that may result in erroneous bearing information. Disturbances result from factors such as lightning, precipitation static, etc. At night, radio beacons are vulnerable to interference from distant stations.

10. **What operational procedure should be used when navigation or approaches are conducted using an NDB?** (AIM 1-1-2)

    Since ADF receivers do not incorporate signal flags to warn a pilot when erroneous bearing information is being displayed, the pilot should continuously monitor the NDBs coded identification.

11. **What is an HSI?** (AC61-27, Ch. 4)

    The horizontal situation indicator is a combination of two instruments, a vertical heading indicator and a VOR/ILS indicator. The aircraft heading is displayed under the upper lubber line. A course indicating arrow shows the course selected (head) and the reciprocal (tail). The course deviation bar operates with a VOR/LOC navigation receiver to indicate left or right deviations for the course selected. The fixed aircraft symbol and course deviation bar display the aircraft relative to the selected course as though you were above the aircraft looking down. The triangular-shaped pointer is the TO-FROM indicator. The glide slope deviation pointer indicates the relation of the aircraft to the glide slope.

12. What is an RMI? (AC 61-27, Ch. 4)

The radio magnetic indicator consists of a rotating compass card, a double-barred bearing indicator, and a single-barred bearing indicator. The compass card, actuated by the compass system, rotates as the aircraft turns. The bearing pointers display ADF or VOR magnetic bearings to the selected station. In most installations, the double-barred bearing indicator gives the magnetic bearing to the VOR or VORTAC and the single-barred indicator is an ADF needle which gives the magnetic bearing to the selected low-frequency facility.

The tail of the double-barred indicator tells you the radial you are on, and the tail of the single-barred indicator tells you your magnetic bearing from a low-frequency station.

13. What is DME? (AIM 1-1-7)

DME stands for *Distance Measuring Equipment*. Aircraft equipped with DME are provided with distance and ground speed information when receiving a VORTAC or TACAN facility. In the operation of DME, paired pulses at a specific spacing are sent out from the aircraft and are received at the ground station. The ground station then transmits paired pulses back to the aircraft at the same pulse spacing but on a different frequency. The time required for the round trip of this signal exchange is measured in the airborne DME unit and is translated into distance and ground speed. Reliable signals may be received at distances up to 199 NM at line-of-sight altitude. DME operates on frequencies in the UHF spectrum between 962 MHz and 1213 MHz. Distance information is slant-range distance, not horizontal.

14. When is DME equipment required? (14 CFR 91.205)

If VOR navigational equipment is required for flight at and above
FL240, the aircraft must be equipped with approved distance
measuring equipment. If the DME should fail at and above FL240,
the pilot-in-command shall notify ATC immediately, and then may
continue operations to the next airport of intended landing where
repairs or equipment replacement can be done.

15. As a rule of thumb, to minimize DME slant range error, how far from the facility should you be to consider the reading accurate? (AC 61-27, Ch. 7)

Slant range error will be at a minimum if the aircraft is one or
more miles from the facility for each 1,000 feet of altitude above
the facility.

16. What is RNAV? (Pilot/Controller Glossary)

RNAV is an abbreviation for *Area Navigation*. It is a form of
navigation that permits aircraft, properly equipped, to operate on
any desired course within the coverage of station-referenced
navigation signals. This form of navigation allows a pilot to select
a more direct course to a destination by not requiring overflight of
ground-based navigational aids. Navigation is to selected
"waypoints" instead of VORs. A "waypoint" is created by simply
moving the VOR to a point along the route of flight desired.

17. What is LORAN? (AIM 1-1-16)

LORAN is an abbreviation for Long Range Navigation. It is an
electronic navigation system by which hyperbolic lines of position
are determined by measuring the difference in the time of reception
of synchronized pulse signals from two fixed transmitters. A
LORAN receiver is basically an onboard computer capable of
determining an aircraft's position based on the measurement of
time-difference receipt of these different signals. LORAN receiv-
ers also have computer memory capable of storing information and
useful programs such as airport locations, navigational aids, etc.,
and programs such as estimated time to station, ground speed, true
airspeed, bearing to nearest airport, etc.

18. What is GPS? (Pilot/Controller Glossary)

Global Positioning System: A space-based radio positioning, navigation, and time transfer system. Provides highly accurate position
and velocity information, and precise time, on a continuous global
basis to an unlimited number of properly-equipped users.

19. Discuss how GPS works. (Pilot/Controller Glossary)

GPS depends on accurate and continuous knowledge of the spatial
position of each system satellite, with respect to time and distance
from a transmitting satellite to the user. The GPS receiver automatically selects appropriate signals from the satellites in view,
translating them into 3-dimensional position, velocity, and time.

20. Is use of GPS navigational equipment approved for IFR operations? (AIM 1-1-21)

The FAA has granted approval for U.S. civil operators to use
properly certified GPS equipment as a primary means of navigation in oceanic airspace and certain remote areas. Properly certified
GPS equipment may be used as a supplemental means of IFR
navigation for domestic en route, terminal operations and certain
instrument approach procedures. Aircraft using GPS navigation
equipment under IFR must be equipped with an approved and
operational alternate means of navigation appropriate to the flight.

I. Airway Route System

1. What are the designated altitudes for the airways in the VOR and L/MF Airway System? (AIM 5-3-4)

The VOR and L/MF Airway System consists of airways designated from 1,200 feet above the surface (or in some instances
higher) up to and including 18,000 feet MSL. These airways are
depicted on Enroute Low Altitude Charts.

2. What are the lateral limits of low altitude Federal airways? (14 CFR 71.75)

Each Federal airway includes the airspace within parallel boundary
lines 4 NM each side of the centerline.

3. **How are federal airways depicted on Enroute Low Altitude Charts?** (AIM 5-3-4)

Except in Alaska and coastal North Carolina, the VOR airways are predicated solely on VOR or VORTAC navigation aids; they are depicted in blue on aeronautical charts (black on Enroute Low Altitude Charts), and are identified by a "V" (Victor) followed by an airway number. A segment of an airway which is common to two or more routes carries the numbers of all the airways which coincide for that segment.

4. **What is a "changeover point"?** (AIM 5-3-6)

It is a point along the route or airway segment between two adjacent navigational facilities or waypoints where changeover in navigational guidance should occur.

5. **What is a "waypoint"?** (Pilot/Controller Glossary)

A "waypoint" is a predetermined geographical position used for route/instrument approach definition, or progress reporting purposes, that is defined relative to a VORTAC station or in terms of latitude/longitude coordinates.

6. **Are the courses depicted on an Enroute Low Altitude Chart magnetic or true courses?** (AC 61-27C, Ch. 13)

They are magnetic courses.

7. **Describe the climb procedure when approaching a fix beyond which a higher MEA exists.**

A pilot may begin a climb to the new MEA at the fix.

8. **Describe the climb procedure when approaching a fix at which a MCA exists.**

A pilot should begin a climb when approaching the fix, in order to arrive at that fix at the MCA. A Minimum Crossing Altitude is the minimum altitude at which certain radio facilities or intersections must be crossed in specified directions of flight. An MCA is

specified if a normal climb, commenced immediately after passing
a fix beyond which a higher MEA applies, would not ensure
adequate obstruction clearance.

**9. VHF/UHF and LF/MF route data will be depicted in
what specific colors on Enroute Low Altitude Charts?**
(Enroute Low Altitude Chart Legend)

VHF/UHF .... Black
LF/MF .... Brown

**10. For the following terms, identify the symbols which
correspond to them on Enroute Low Altitude Charts.**
*(These symbols might not all be on your Enroute Low
Altitude Chart.)*

VOR/DME ....

TACAN ....

VOR ....

VORTAC ....

NDB ....

Commercial broadcast station ....

Compass locator frequency ....

Localizer facility information box ....

VORTAC facility information box .... (blue)

Controlling FSS ....

Remote air/ground communications with ARTCC ....

Continued

Airport with a published instrument approach .... *(see below)*

Airport without a published instrument approach .... *(see below)*

AIRPORT DATA	Airports/Seaplane bases shown in BLUE and GREEN have an approved Low Altitude Instrument Approach Procedure published. Those in BLUE have an approved DOD Low Altitude Instrument Approach Procedure and/or DOD RADAR MINIMA published in DOD FLIPS or Alaska Terminal. Airports/Seaplane bases shown in BROWN do not have a published Instrument Approach Procedure.

Compass rose ....

ATC compulsory reporting point ....

ATC noncompulsory reporting point ....

DME fix distance when not obvious ....

DME fix distance when the same as route miles ....

VOR changeover point ....

Mileage break at an airway course change, intersection,

or breakdown point .... *(see diagram)*

Mileage between VORs or a VOR and compulsory

reporting point ....

Victor airway ....

ARTCC boundary, controlling ARTCC.....................

MOCA ....

MEA ....

Change in MEA or MOCA at other than NAVAIDs ......

Minimum Crossing Altitude .... MCA
V6 4000S

Minimum Reception Altitude .... MRA 9000

Maximum Authorized Altitude MAA-15500 **V30** MAA-15500 (R5)

Magnetic variation .... 7°E

Control zone boundary (Class D or E airspace) ....

Special-use airspace .... *(see below)*

AIRSPACE INFORMATION

SPECIAL USE AIRSPACE

Only the airspace effective below 18,000 feet MSL is shown.

†P-56
W-123
A-123
REESE 1 MOA
R-1234 ①
TO 10000 ②
0600-1800Z
MON-FRI ③
IFR ④
FSS ⑤

TO 5000

A - Alert Area
P - Prohibited Area
R - Restricted Area
W - Warning Area
D - Danger Area (Canada)

Line delimits altitude separation within same Special Use Airspace Area

BROWN MOA
8000 AND ABOVE
INTERMITTENT
BY NOTAM
KANSAS CITY CENTER/FSS

Special Air Traffic Rules

MOA - Military Operations Area

†Indicates complete information in tabulation on front panel

SPECIAL USE AIRSPACE WILL INCLUDE:

① AREA IDENTIFICATION: In Canada area ident is preceded by the letters CY (CANADA) followed by a number (PROVINCE).

② EFFECTIVE ALTITUDE CEILINGS ARE SHOWN UP TO BUT NOT INCLUDING 18,000'. WHEN THE AIRSPACE ENCOMPASSES ALL ALTITUDES IN THE LOW ALTITUDE STRUCTURE, NO ALTITUDE WILL BE SHOWN. THE WORK "TO" (AN ALTITUDE) MEANS "TO AND INCLUDING" (THAT ALTITUDE).

③ OPERATING TIME: When continuous no time is shown.
Days: Sunrise to Sunset.
Nights: Sunset to Sunrise.
Hours: Given in UTC; e.g., 0600-1300Z
Mon-Fri: Indicates area does not exist on Sat. or Sun.

1 Mar.-15 June: Indicates area in use only through dates given. By NOTAM: Area activated by NOTAM. Days are local.

④ Weather Conditions during which the area is in operation. When continuous no weather is shown.
VFR: Used only during VFR conditions. IFR: Used only during IFR conditions.

⑤ Voice Call of Controlling Agency for enroute clearance through area. No A/G unless indicated.

Class B airspace ....

Class C airspace ....

AIRSPACE INFORMATION

Class E airspace ....

Open area (white) indicates controlled
airspace (Class E) unless otherwise
indicated.
All airspace 14,500' and above is
controlled (Class E).

Class G airspace ....

Shaded area (brown) indicates
uncontrolled airspace below 14,500'
(Class G).

Mode C area ....

ARTCC boundaries ....

ARTCC Remoted VHF/UHF frequency site ....

NAME
Name
000.0   000.0

Air Defense Identification Zone (ADIZ) ....

HIWAS .... ■

TWEB .... ❶

ILS localizer course with ATC function

ATIS ....

(Airport Name) [D]
280 (L)* 43s
(A)   *109.8

Automatic Terminal
Information Service

Pilot Controlled Lighting .... (L)

Special VFR not authorized .... No SVFR

J. Airspace

1. What is Class A airspace? (AIM 3-2-2)

Generally, that airspace from 18,000 feet MSL up to and including FL600, including airspace overlying the waters within 12 nautical miles of the coast of the 48 contiguous states and Alaska; and designated international airspace beyond 12 nautical miles of the coast of the 48 contiguous states and Alaska within areas of domestic radio navigational signal or ATC radar coverage, and within which domestic procedures are applied.

2. What is Class B airspace? (AIM 3-2-3)

Generally, that airspace from the surface to 10,000 feet MSL surrounding the nation's busiest airports in terms of IFR operations or passenger enplanements. The configuration of each Class B airspace area is individually tailored and consists of a surface area and two or more layers (some resemble upside-down wedding cakes), and is designated to contain all published instrument procedures once an aircraft enters the airspace. An ATC clearance is required for all aircraft to operate in the area, and all aircraft cleared as such receive separation services within the airspace. The cloud clearance requirement for VFR operations is "clear of clouds."

3. What is Class C airspace? (AIM 3-2-4)

Generally, that airspace from the surface to 4,000 feet above the airport elevation (charted in MSL) surrounding airports that have an operational control tower, are serviced by a radar approach control, and that have a certain number of IFR operations or passenger enplanements. Although the configuration of each Class C airspace area is individually tailored, the airspace usually consists of a 5 NM radius core surface area that extends from the surface up to 4,000 feet above the airport elevation, and a 10 NM radius shelf area that extends from 1,200 feet to 4,000 feet above the airport elevation.

4. What is Class D airspace? (AIM 3-2-5)

Generally, that airspace from the surface to 2,500 feet above the airport elevation (charted in MSL) surrounding airports that have an operational control tower. The configuration of each Class D airspace area is individually tailored, and when instrument procedures are published, the airspace will usually be designed to contain those procedures.

5. When a control tower, located at an airport within Class D airspace, ceases operation for the day, what happens to the lower limit of the controlled airspace? (AIM 3-2-5)

During the hours the tower is not in operation, Class E surface area rules, or a combination of Class E rules to 700 feet AGL and Class G rules to the surface, will become applicable. Check the A/FD for specifics.

6. What is Class E (controlled) airspace? (AIM 3-2-6)

Generally, if the airspace is not Class A, Class B, Class C, or Class D, and it is controlled airspace, it is Class E airspace. Class E airspace extends upward from either the surface or a designated altitude to the overlying controlled airspace. When designated as a surface area, the airspace will be configured to contain all instrument procedures. Also in this class are Federal airways, airspace beginning at either 700 or 1,200 feet AGL used to transition to or from the terminal or enroute environment, enroute domestic, and offshore airspace areas designated below 18,000 feet MSL. Unless designated at a lower altitude, Class E airspace begins at 14,500 feet MSL over the United States, including that airspace overlying the waters within 12 nautical miles of the coast of the 48 contiguous states and Alaska, up to, but not including 18,000 feet MSL, and the airspace above FL600.

7. What is the floor of Class E airspace when designated in conjunction with an airport with an approved IAP? (14 CFR 71.71)

700 feet AGL.

8. **What is the floor of Class E airspace when designated in conjunction with a federal airway?** (14 CFR 71.71)

1,200 feet AGL.

9. **Class E airspace within the contiguous United States extends upward from either 700 feet AGL or 1,200 feet AGL, up to but not including what altitude?** (AIM 3-2-6)

Except for 18,000 feet MSL, Class E airspace has no defined vertical limit; rather, it extends upward from either the surface or a designated altitude to the overlying or adjacent controlled airspace. Unless designated at a lower altitude, Class E airspace begins at 14,500 feet MSL and extends up to, but not including 18,000 feet MSL, overlying the 48 contiguous states including the waters within 12 miles from the coast of the contiguous states.

10. **What is Class G airspace?** (AIM 3-3-1)

Class G airspace is that portion of the airspace that has not been designated as Class A, B, C, D, and E airspace.

11. **What are the vertical limits of Class G airspace?**

Class G airspace begins at the surface and continues up to but not including the overlying controlled airspace, or 14,500 MSL, or where Class E airspace begins, whichever occurs first.

K. Special Use Airspace

1. **Define the following types of airspace.**
   (AIM 3-4-1 through 3-4-7 and 3-5-7)

Prohibited Area—For security or other reasons, aircraft flight is prohibited.

Restricted Area—Contains unusual, often invisible hazards to aircraft, flights must have permission from the controlling agency, if VFR. IFR flights will be cleared through or vectored around it.

Continued

Military Operations Area—MOAs consist of airspace of defined vertical and lateral limits established for the purpose of separating certain military training activities from IFR traffic. Permission is not required for VFR flights, but extreme caution should be exercised. IFR flights will be cleared through or vectored around it.

Warning Area—Airspace of defined dimensions extending from 3 nautical miles outward from the coast of the U.S. containing activity that may be hazardous to nonparticipating aircraft. A warning area may be located over domestic or international waters or both. Permission is not required but a flight plan is advised.

Alert Area—Depicted on aeronautical charts to inform nonparticipating pilots of areas that may contain a high volume of pilot training or an unusual type of aerial activity. No permission is required, but VFR flights should exercise extreme caution. IFR flights will be cleared through or vectored around it.

Controlled Firing Areas—CFAs contain activities which, if not conducted in a controlled environment, could be hazardous to nonparticipating aircraft. These activities are suspended immediately when spotter aircraft, radar or ground lookout positions, indicate an aircraft might be approaching the area. CFAs are not charted.

National Security Area—Airspace of defined vertical and lateral dimensions established at locations where there is a requirement for increased security and safety of ground facilities. Pilots are requested to voluntarily avoid flying through the depicted NSA. When it is necessary to provide a greater level of security and safety, flight in NSAs may be temporarily prohibited by regulation under the provisions of 14 CFR 99.7.

2. Where can information on special use airspace be found?

The chart legend contains information on special use airspace such as times of use, altitudes, and the controlling agency.

L. Physiological Factors

1. What is hypoxia? (AIM 8-1-2)

Hypoxia is a state of oxygen deficiency in the body sufficient to impair functions of the brain and other organs.

2. What factors can make you more susceptible to hypoxia? (AIM 8-1-2)

Alcohol, low doses of certain drugs (such as antihistamines, tranquilizers, sedatives, and analgesics), and cigarette smoking make a pilot more susceptible to hypoxia.

3. For optimum protection against hypoxia, when should pilots use supplemental oxygen? (AIM 8-1-2)

During daylight hours .... above 10,000 feet
At night .... above 5,000 feet

4. What is hyperventilation? (AIM 8-1-3)

Hyperventilation is an abnormal increase in the volume of air breathed in and out of the lungs. It causes an excessive loss of carbon dioxide from the body. Symptoms are lightheadedness, drowsiness, and tingling in the extremities.

5. What is recommended if hyperventilation is suspected? (AIM 8-1-3)

The rate and depth of breathing should be consciously slowed down. Controlled breathing in and out of a paper bag can build carbon dioxide back to a normal level.

6. What is carbon monoxide poisoning? (AIM 8-1-4)

Carbon monoxide is a colorless, odorless, tasteless gas contained in exhaust fumes. Most heaters in light aircraft work by air flowing over the exhaust manifold. Cracks may form in the manifold, causing carbon monoxide to leak into the cockpit.

7. **What are symptoms of carbon monoxide poisoning and what action should be taken if it is suspected?** (AIM 8-1-4)

Some symptoms are headache, drowsiness, and dizziness. If carbon monoxide poisoning is suspected, shut the heater off, and open the air vents.

Arrival 4

A. Approach Control

1. What is a STAR? (AIM 5-4-1)

A *Standard Terminal Arrival Route* (STAR) is an ATC-coded IFR
arrival route established for use by arriving IFR aircraft destined
for certain airports. Its purpose is to simplify clearance delivery
procedures and facilitate transition between enroute and instrument
approach procedures. Reference the Terminal Procedures Publication (TPP) for the availability of STARs.

2. If ATC issues your flight a STAR, must you accept it? (AIM 5-4-1)

You are not required to accept a STAR, but if you do, you must
have an approved textual description available. Recommended
action if a STAR is not desired is to place "NO STAR" in the
Remarks section of the IFR flight plan.

3. When being radar-vectored for an approach, at what point may you start a descent from your last assigned altitude to a lower altitude if "cleared for the approach"? (AIM 5-5-4)

When "cleared for the approach" the pilot may begin descent from
last assigned altitude when established on a segment of a published
route or instrument approach procedure.

4. Define the terms:
Initial approach segment
Intermediate approach segment
Final approach segment
Missed approach segment
(Pilot/Controller Glossary)

An instrument approach procedure may have as many as four
separate segments, depending on how the approach procedure
is structured.

Continued

The *initial approach segment* is that segment of an instrument approach procedure between the initial approach fix and the intermediate approach fix or, where applicable, the final approach fix or point.

The *intermediate approach segment* is that segment of an instrument approach procedure between either the intermediate approach fix and the final approach fix or point, or between the end of a reversal, race track, or dead reckoning track procedure and the final approach fix or point, as appropriate.

The *final approach segment* is that segment of an instrument approach procedure in which alignment and descent for landing are accomplished.

The *missed approach segment* is the segment between the missed approach point or the point of arrival at decision height and the missed approach fix at the prescribed altitude.

5. What obstacle clearance are you normally guaranteed during the initial, intermediate, final, and missed approach segments of a standard instrument approach procedure?

The initial approach segment provides 1,000-foot obstacle clearance when within 4 miles either side of course.

The intermediate approach segment provides 500-foot obstacle clearance within a protected area tapering uniformly from the initial approach segment to the width of the final approach course.

The final approach segment obstacle clearance depends on the type of approach. ILS approaches have the least, with 190 feet being the standard. NDB approaches require the most obstacle clearance, usually being as much as 350 feet. The width of the obstacle clearance area depends on the type of approach as well as the length of the final approach course.

6. What is a Minimum Vectoring Altitude (MVA)?
(Pilot/Controller Glossary and AIM 5-4-5)

MVA is the lowest MSL altitude at which an IFR aircraft will be vectored by a radar controller, except as otherwise authorized for radar approaches, departures, and missed approaches. The altitude meets IFR obstacle clearance criteria. It may be lower than the published MEA along an airway or J-route segment. It may be used for radar vectoring only upon the controller's determination that an adequate radar return is being received from the aircraft being controlled. Charts depicting minimum vectoring altitudes are normally available only to the controllers and not to the pilots.

7. How does a pilot navigate between the enroute phase and the initial approach segment? (AIM 5-4-6, 5-4-7)

In this case navigation is accomplished by feeder routes or radar vectors. Feeder routes are depicted on approach procedure charts to designate routes for aircraft to proceed from the enroute structure to the initial approach fix. All routes will include a minimum altitude, course, and distance.

8. What procedure is to be used when the clearance "cleared for the visual" is issued? (AIM 5-4-20)

A visual approach is conducted on an IFR flight plan and authorizes a pilot to proceed visually and clear of clouds to the airport. The pilot must have either the airport or the preceding identified aircraft in sight. This approach must be authorized and controlled by the appropriate air traffic control facility. Reported weather at the airport must have a ceiling at or above 1,000 feet and visibility 3 miles or greater.

Visual approaches are an IFR procedure conducted under IFR in visual meteorological conditions. Cloud clearance requirements of 14 CFR 91.155 are not applicable.

9. Describe the term "contact approach."
(Pilot/Controller Glossary)

An approach in which an aircraft on an IFR flight plan, having an air traffic control authorization, operating clear of clouds with at least 1 mile flight visibility and a reasonable expectation of continuing to the destination airport in those conditions, may deviate from the instrument approach procedure and proceed to the destination airport by visual reference to the surface. This approach will only be authorized when requested by the pilot and the reported ground visibility at the destination airport is at least 1 statute mile.

10. When is a procedure turn not required? (AIM 5-4-8)

A procedure turn is not required when:

a. The symbol "NoPT" is depicted.

b. "Radar Vectoring" is provided.

c. A holding pattern is published in lieu of a procedure turn.

d. Conducting a timed approach.

e. The procedure turn is not authorized (absence of procedure turn barb on plan view).

11. What are standard procedure turn limitations? (AIM 5-4-8)

a. Turn on the depicted side.

b. Adhere to depicted minimum altitudes.

c. Complete the maneuver within the distance specified in the profile view.

d. Maneuver at a maximum speed not greater than 200 knots (IAS).

12. What procedure is followed when a holding pattern is specified in lieu of a procedure turn? (AIM 5-4-8)

A holding pattern, in lieu of a procedure turn, may be specified for course reversal in some procedures: the holding pattern is established over an intermediate fix or final approach fix. The holding pattern distance or time specified in the profile view must be observed. Maximum holding airspeed limitations apply, as set forth for all holding patterns. The holding pattern maneuver is completed when the aircraft is established on the inbound course after executing the appropriate entry. If cleared for the approach prior to returning to the holding fix, and the aircraft is at the prescribed altitude, additional circuits of the holding pattern are not necessary nor expected by ATC. If pilots elect to make additional circuits to lose altitude or to become better established on course, it is their responsibility to so advise ATC upon receipt of their approach clearance.

B. Precision Approaches

1. Define a precision approach. (Pilot/Controller Glossary)

A precision approach is a standard instrument approach procedure in which an electronic glide slope/glide path is provided. Examples are: ILS, MLS, and PAR.

2. What are the basic components of a standard ILS? (AIM 1-1-9)

Guidance information .... localizer, glide slope

Range information .... marker beacons, DME

Visual information .... approach lights, touchdown and centerline lights, runway lights

3. Describe both visual and aural indications that a pilot would receive when crossing the outer, middle, and inner markers of a standard ILS. (AIM 1-1-9)

Outer Marker	**Middle Marker**	**Inner Marker**
blue light	amber light	white light
dull tone	medium tone	high tone
slow speed	medium speed	high speed
– – – – – –	– . – . – .	. . . . . .

4. What are the distances from the landing threshold of the outer, middle, and inner markers? (AIM 1-1-9)

Outer marker .... 4 to 7 miles from threshold

Middle marker .... 3,500 feet from threshold

Inner marker .... between middle marker and threshold

5. When is the inner marker used? (AIM 1-1-9)

Ordinarily, there are two marker beacons associated with an ILS, the outer marker (OM) and middle marker (MM). Locations with a Category II ILS also have an inner marker (IM).

6. **To maintain glide slope and desired airspeed on an ILS approach, how are power and pitch used?** (AC 61-27C, Ch. 5)

   When on the final segment of an ILS final approach, change pitch to control glide path, and change power to control airspeed.

7. **While flying a 3° glide slope, which conditions should the pilot expect concerning airspeed, pitch attitude and altitude when encountering a windshear situation where a tailwind shears to a calm or headwind?** (AC 00-54)

   Pitch attitude .... Increase
   Required thrust .... Reduced, then increased
   Vertical speed .... Decreases, then increases
   Airspeed .... Increases, then decreases
   Reaction .... Reduce power initially, then increase

8. **While flying a 3° glide slope, which conditions should the pilot expect concerning airspeed, pitch attitude, and altitude when encountering a windshear situation where a headwind shears to a calm or tailwind?** (AC 00-54)

   Pitch attitude .... Decrease
   Required thrust .... Increased, then reduced
   Vertical speed .... Increases
   Airspeed .... Decreases, then increases
   Reaction .... Increased power, then a decrease in power

9. **Localizers operate within what frequency range?** (AIM 1-1-9)

   Localizers operate on odd tenths within the 108.10 to 111.95 MHz band.

10. **Where is the localizer/transmitter antenna installation located in relation to the runway?** (AIM 1-1-9)

    The antenna is located at the far end of the approach runway.

11. Where is the glide slope antenna located and what is its normal usable range? (AIM 1-1-9)

The glide slope transmitter is located between 750 feet and 1,250 feet from the approach end of the runway (down the runway), and offset 250 feet to 650 feet from it. The glide slope is normally usable to a distance of 10 NM.

12. What range does a standard localizer have? (AIM 1-1-9)

The localizer signal provides course guidance throughout the descent path to the runway threshold from a distance of 18 NM from the antenna site.

13. What is the angular width of a localizer signal? (AIM 1-1-9)

The localizer signal is adjusted to provide an angular width of between $3°$ to $6°$, as necessary to provide a linear width of 700 feet at the runway approach threshold.

14. What is the normal glide slope angle for a standard ILS? (AIM 1-1-9)

The glide path projection angle is normally 3 degrees above horizontal so that it intersects the MM at about 200 feet and the OM at about 1,400 feet above the runway elevation.

15. What is the sensitivity of a CDI tuned to a localizer signal compared with a CDI tuned to a VOR? (AIM 1-1-9)

Full left or full right deflection occurs at approximately $2.5°$ from the centerline of a localizer course, which is 4 times greater than when tuned to a VOR, where full-scale deflection equals $10°$ from the centerline.

16. Define the term "decision height" (DH). (14 CFR Part 1)

With respect to the operation of an aircraft, decision height means the height at which a decision must be made, during an ILS, MLS, or PAR instrument approach to either continue the approach or execute a missed approach.

17. When flying an instrument approach procedure, when can the pilot descend below the MDA or DH?
(14 CFR 91.175)

No person may operate an aircraft below the prescribed MDA or continue an approach below the authorized DH unless:

a. The aircraft is continuously in a position from which a descent to a landing on the intended runway can be made at a normal rate of descent using normal maneuvers.

b. The flight visibility is not less than the visibility prescribed in the standard instrument approach procedure being used.

c. When at least one of the following visual references for the intended runway is distinctly visible and identifiable to the pilot:

- The approach light system, (except that the pilot may not descend below 100 feet above the touchdown zone elevation using the ALS as a reference unless the red terminating bars or the red side row bars are also distinctly visible and identifiable)
- The threshold
- The threshold markings
- The threshold lights
- REIL
- VASI
- The touchdown zone markings
- The touchdown zone lights
- The runway and runway markings
- The runway lights

18. **What are the legal substitutes for an ILS outer marker and middle marker?** (14 CFR 91.175)

Outer marker: Compass locator, PAR, ASR or the DME, VOR and NDB fixes authorized in the instrument approach procedure.

Middle marker: Compass locators or PAR are the only legal substitutions.

19. **If the middle marker is out of service for a particular ILS procedure, will the minimums change, and if so, how much?**

For Part 91 operators, there is no longer an increase in DH when the middle marker is inoperative.

20. **What are PAR and ASR approaches?** (AIM 5-4-10)

A PAR approach is a type of radar approach in which a controller provides highly accurate navigational guidance in azimuth and elevation to the pilot (precision approach). An ASR approach is a type of radar approach in which a controller provides navigational guidance in azimuth only (nonprecision approach).

21. **What is a "no-gyro" approach?**
(Pilot/Controller Glossary; AIM 5-4-10)

A "no-gyro" approach is a radar approach/vector provided in case of a malfunctioning gyro-compass or directional gyro. Instead of providing the pilot with headings to be flown, the controller observes the radar track and issues control instructions "Turn right/ left," or "Stop turn," as appropriate.

22. **What rate of turn is recommended during execution of a "no-gyro" approach procedure?** (AIM 5-4-10)

On a no-gyro approach, all turns should be standard rate until on final; then one-half standard rate on final approach.

23. If conducting an ASR approach, are the minimums expressed as DH or MDA? (AIM 5-4-10)

An ASR approach is a nonprecision approach with no glide slope provided; minimums are depicted as MDA.

C. Nonprecision Approaches

1. What is a nonprecision approach?
(Pilot/Controller Glossary)

It is a standard instrument approach procedure in which no glide slope is provided.

2. Name the types of nonprecision approach procedures available. (Pilot/Controller Glossary)

The types of nonprecision approaches available are VOR, TACAN, NDB, LOC, ASR, LDA, and SDF.

3. Define MDA. (Pilot/Controller Glossary)

The Minimum Descent Altitude is the lowest altitude, expressed in feet above MSL, to which descent is authorized on final approach or during circle-to-land maneuvering, in execution of a standard instrument approach procedure where no electronic glide slope is provided.

4. Define VDP. (Pilot/Controller Glossary)

Visual Descent Point—a VDP is a defined point on the final approach course of a nonprecision straight-in approach procedure from which normal descent from the MDA to the runway touch-down point may be commenced, provided the approach threshold of that runway, or approach lights or other markings identifiable with the approach end of that runway, are clearly visible to the pilot. Pilots not equipped to receive the VDP should fly the approach procedure as though no VDP had been provided.

5. **Will standard instrument approach procedures always have a Final Approach Fix (FAF)?** (AC 61-27C)

No, NDB and VOR approaches with the primary navigational aid on the field will not always have a designated FAF.

6. **If no FAF is published, where does the final approach segment begin on a nonprecision approach?** (AC 61-27C)

The final approach segment begins where the procedure turn intersects the final approach course inbound.

7. **Certain conditions are required for an instrument approach procedure to have "straight-in" minimums published. What are they?** (AIM 5-4-18)

Straight-in minimums are shown on the IAP when the final approach course is within 30 degrees of the runway alignment and a normal descent can be made from the IFR altitude shown on the IAP to the runway surface.

8. **What is a stepdown fix?** (Pilot/Controller Glossary)

A stepdown fix permits additional descent within a segment of an instrument approach procedure by identifying a point at which a controlling obstacle has been safely overflown.

9. **What does a VASI system provide?** (AIM 2-1-2)

A VASI system provides visual descent guidance during an approach to a runway; safe obstacle clearance within ±10° of extended runway centerline up to 4 NM from the runway; and a 3° glide slope.

10. What are the major differences between SDF and LDA approaches? (AC 61-27C, Ch. 7)

In an SDF approach procedure, the SDF course may or may not be aligned with the runway; usable off-course indications are limited to 35° either side of course centerline. The SDF signal emitted is fixed at either 6° or 12°.

In the LDA approach procedure the LDA course is of comparable utility and accuracy to a standard localizer. An LDA course is usually not aligned with the runway; however, straight-in minimums may be published where the angle between the centerline and course does not exceed 30°. If the angle exceeds 30°, only circling minimums are published.

11. What criteria determines whether or not you may attempt an approach? (14 CFR 91.175)

No regulation states that you cannot attempt an approach, if operating under Part 91 regulations. But if you reach MDA or DH and decide to descend to land, flight visibility must be at least equal to that published.

12. What regulations require use of specified procedures by all pilots approaching for landing under IFR? (14 CFR Part 97)

Specified procedures are required by 14 CFR Part 97.

D. Circling Approaches

1. What are circle-to-land approaches?
(Pilot/Controller Glossary)

A circle-to-land approach is not technically an approach, but a maneuver initiated by a pilot to align the aircraft with the runway for landing when a straight-in landing from an instrument approach is not possible or desirable. The maneuver is made only when authorized by ATC and visual reference with the airport is established and maintained.

2. Why do certain airports have only circling minimums published? (AIM 5-4-18)

When either the normal rate of descent from MDA would be excessive or the runway alignment exceeds 30°, a straight-in minimum is not published and a circling minimum applies.

3. Can a pilot make a straight-in landing if using an approach procedure having only circling minimums? (AIM 5-4-18)

Yes; the fact that a straight-in minimum is not published does not preclude pilots from landing straight-in, if they have the active runway in sight and have sufficient time to make a normal approach to landing. Under such conditions and when ATC has cleared them for landing on that runway, pilots are not expected to circle, even though only circling minimums are published.

4. If cleared for a "straight-in VOR-DME 34 approach," can a pilot circle to land, if needed? (Pilot/Controller Glossary)

Yes, a "straight-in approach" is an instrument approach wherein final approach is begun without first having executed a procedure turn. Such an approach is not necessarily completed with a straight-in landing or made to straight-in minimums.

5. When can you begin your descent to the runway during a circling approach? (14 CFR 91.175)

Three conditions are required before descent from the MDA can occur:

a. The aircraft is continuously in a position from which a descent to a landing on the intended runway can be made at a normal rate of descent using normal maneuvers.

b. The flight visibility is not less than the visibility prescribed in the standard instrument approach being used.

c. At least one of the specific runway visual references for the intended runway is distinctly visible and identifiable to the pilot.

6. **While circling to land you lose visual contact with the runway environment. At the time visual contact is lost, your approximate position is a base leg at the circling MDA. What procedure should be followed?** (AIM 5-4-19)

If visual reference is lost while circling to land from an instrument approach, the pilot should make an initial climbing turn toward the landing runway and continue the turn until established on the missed approach course. Since the circling maneuver may be accomplished in more than one direction, different patterns will be required to become established on the prescribed missed approach course, depending on the aircraft position at the time visual reference is lost. Adherence to the procedure will ensure that an aircraft will remain within the circling and missed approach obstacle clearance areas.

7. **What obstacle clearance are you guaranteed during a circling approach maneuver?** (AIM Fig. 5-4-7)

In all circling approaches, the circling minimum provides 300 feet of obstacle clearance within the circling approach area. The size of this area depends on the category in which the aircraft operates.

Category A .... 1.3-mile radius
Category B .... 1.5-mile radius
Category C .... 1.7-mile radius
Category D .... 2.3-mile radius
Category E .... 4.5-mile radius

8. **How can a pilot determine the approach category minimums applicable to a particular aircraft?**
(14 CFR Part 97)

Minimums are specified for various aircraft speed/weight combinations. Speeds are based upon a value 1.3 times the stalling speed of the aircraft in the landing configuration (V_{S0}) at a maximum certificated gross landing weight.

9. **What are the different aircraft approach categories?**
(14 CFR 97.3)

Category A .... Speed less than 91 knots
Category B .... Speed 91 knots or more but less than 121 knots
Category C .... Speed 121 knots or more but less than 141 knots
Category D .... Speed 141 knots or more but less than 166 knots
Category E .... Speed 166 knots or more

10. **An aircraft operating under 14 CFR Part 91 has a 1.3 times V_{S0} speed of 100 KIAS, making Category B minimums applicable. If it becomes necessary to circle at a speed in excess of this category, what minimums should be used?**

An aircraft can only fit into one approach category. If it is necessary to maneuver at speeds in excess of the upper limit of the speed range for each category, the minimum for the next higher approach category should be used.

E. Missed Approaches

1. **When must a pilot execute a missed approach?**
(AIM 5-5-5)

A missed approach must be executed when one of the following conditions occurs:

a. Arrival at the missed approach point and the runway environment is not yet in sight,

b. Arrival at DH on the glide slope with the runway environment not yet in sight,

c. Anytime a pilot determines a safe landing is not possible,

d. When circling-to-land visual contact is lost,

e. When instructed by ATC.

2. On a nonprecision approach procedure, how is the Missed Approach Point (MAP) determined? (AC 61-27C, Ch. 12)

The pilot normally determines the MAP by timing from the final approach fix. The MAP may also be determined through use of DME or a specific fix utilizing VOR, ADF, or RNAV if authorized on the approach chart.

3. Where, geographically, does the MAP on a straight-in nonprecision approach occur? (AC 61-27C, Ch. 12)

The MAP on a nonprecision approach usually occurs over the runway threshold.

4. If no final approach fix is depicted, how is the MAP determined? (AC 61-27C, Ch. 10, p. 186)

The MAP is at the airport (NAVAID on airport).

5. Where is the MAP on a precision approach? (AC 61-27C, Ch. 12)

On a precision approach, the MAP is at the DH on glide slope.

6. Under what conditions are missed approach procedures published on an approach chart not followed? (AC 61-27C, Ch. 12)

They are not followed when ATC has assigned alternate missed approach instructions.

7. If, during the execution of an instrument approach procedure, you determine a missed approach is necessary due to full-scale needle deflection, what action is recommended? (AIM 5-4-19)

Protected obstacle clearance areas for missed approach are predicated on the assumption that the abort is initiated at MAP, not lower than MDA or DH. Reasonable buffers are provided for normal maneuvers; however, no consideration is given to an abnormally early turn. Therefore, when an early missed approach is executed, pilots should fly the IAP as specified on the approach plate to MAP at or above MDA or DH, before executing a missed approach procedure.

8. What is a low approach? (AIM 4-3-12)

A low approach (sometimes referred to as a low pass) is the go-around maneuver following an approach. Instead of landing or making a touch and go, a pilot may wish to go-around (low approach) in order to expedite a particular operation (a series of practice instrument approaches is an example). Unless otherwise authorized by ATC, the low approach should be made straight ahead, with no turns or climb made until the pilot has made a thorough visual check for other aircraft in the area.

9. What does the phrase "Cleared for the Option" mean? (AIM 4-3-22)

The "Cleared for the Option" procedure will permit an instructor, flight examiner or pilot the option to make a touch-and-go, low approach, missed approach, stop-and-go, or full stop landing. The pilot should make a request for this procedure passing the final approach fix inbound on an instrument approach.

F. Landing Procedures

1. Is it legal to land a civil aircraft if the actual visibility is below the minimums published on the approach chart? (14 CFR 91.175)

No, 14 CFR Part 91 states that no pilot operating an aircraft, except a military aircraft of the U.S., may land that aircraft when the flight visibility is less than the visibility prescribed in the standard instrument approach procedure being used.

2. When landing at an airport with an operating control tower following an IFR flight, must the pilot call FSS to close the flight plan? (AIM 5-1-13)

No, if operating on an IFR flight plan to an airport with a functioning control tower, the flight plan will automatically be closed upon landing.

3. Is the reported ceiling a requirement for landing? (AC 61-27C, Ch. 12)

No, an aircraft may still be in and out of clouds when at DH or MDA, but have the runway environment in sight. Provided the visibility requirement is met, a descent for landing is authorized.

G. Logging Flight Time

1. What conditions are necessary for a pilot to log instrument time? (14 CFR 61.51)

A pilot may log as instrument flight time only that time during which he/she operates the aircraft solely by reference to instruments, under actual or simulated flight conditions.

2. When logging instrument time, what should be included in each entry? (14 CFR 61.51)

Each entry must include the place and type of each instrument approach completed, and the name of the safety pilot (if applicable).

3. What conditions must exist in order to log "actual" instrument flight time?

"Actual" instrument flight time would include any flight time accumulated in IMC conditions. The definition for IMC (Instrument Meteorological Conditions) is meteorological conditions less than the minimum specified for visual meteorological conditions. VFR minimums are found in 14 CFR 91.155.

H. Instrument Approach Procedure Charts: General

All questions in this section reference government NOAA charts.

1. If a particular approach name has a letter "A" attached as a suffix (such as VOR DME A), what does this indicate? (AC 61-27C)

A letter after the approach name indicates that the approach does not meet straight-in criteria and only circling minimums are available.

2. Do all standard instrument approach procedures have final approach fixes? (AC 61-27C)

No, some nonprecision approaches may not have a final approach fix. These particular approaches usually have the NAVAID upon which the approach is based located on the airport.

3. With no FAF available, when would final descent to the published MDA be started? (AC 61-27C)

When flying the full procedure, this is usually started upon completion of the procedure turn and when established on the final approach course inbound. When being radar-vectored to the final approach course, descent shall be accomplished when within the specified distance from the NAVAID and established on the inbound course.

4. Why would an airport with a standard instrument approach procedure available be designated "not authorized" as an alternate?

If an airport is "Not Authorized" as an alternate under any conditions, one of the following usually applies:

a. The NAVAID upon which the approach is based is not monitored by an ATC facility; it could malfunction and possibly shut down without ATC being immediately aware of the condition.

b. The airport does not have approved weather reporting capability.

*The following questions are in reference to the ILS 16L approach
chart for Fort Worth, Texas, depicted on page 4-28 (NOS effective
date April 23, 1998).*

I. Instrument Approach Procedure Charts: Plan View

1. What are the MSAs for this approach? (AC 61-27C)

2,200 feet .... 180° through 270°
3,400 feet .... 270° through 360°
2,800 feet .... 360° through 180°

2. On which facility is the MSA centered, and what does it provide? (AIM 5-4-5)

The MSA is centered on the Mufin LOM; the altitude shown
provides at least 1,000 feet of clearance above the highest obstacle
within the defined sector up to a distance of 25 NM from the
facility. Navigational course guidance is not assured at the MSA.

3. What is the IAF for this procedure? (AC 61-27C)

The IAF is MUFIN LOM.

4. What significance does the bold arrow extending from Bowie VOR have? (AC 61-27C)

It represents a feeder route or flyable route utilized when transi-
tioning from the enroute structure to the initial approach fix.

5. When intercepting the localizer from procedure turn inbound, what will be the relative bearing on the ADF indicator as the localizer needle begins to center? (AC 61-27C)

Assuming a 45° intercept angle, the relative bearing will be 315°.

6. **What are the frequencies for the locator outer marker and middle marker beacons?** (AC 61-27C)

The locator frequency is 365 kHz. All marker beacons transmit on a frequency of 75 MHz.

7. **What significance does the ring labeled "10 NM" and centered on the MUFIN LOM have?** (AC 61-27C)

The ring, normally a 10-NM radius, provides the boundary to scale of the procedure that is charted.

8. **Where does the final approach segment begin for the ILS 16L approach?** (AC 61-27C)

On all precision approaches, the final approach segment begins when the glide slope is intercepted at glide slope altitude. For nonprecision approaches such as the straight-in LOC 16L approach, the final approach segment begins at the maltese cross which is the MUFIN LOM.

J. Instrument Approach Procedure Charts: Profile

1. **Within what distance from the MUFIN LOM must the procedure turn be executed?** (AC 61-27C)

The procedure turn must be executed within 10 NM.

2. **If a procedure turn is required, what would be the minimum altitude while flying this segment?** (AC 61-27C)

The minimum altitude for the initial approach segment and while executing the procedure turn is 2,200 feet MSL.

3. **To what altitude may a pilot descend after the procedure turn?** (AC 61-27C)

When established inbound after the procedure turn, the pilot may descend to 2,000 MSL.

4. What does the number "1991" located at the outer marker indicate? (AC 61-27C)

1991 indicates the altitude of the glide slope at the outer marker.

5. What is the glide slope angle for this approach? (AC 61-27C)

The glide slope angle is 3°.

6. What is the altitude at which the electronic glide slope crosses the threshold of runway 16L? (AC 61-27C)

Threshold crossing height (TCH) is 57 feet.

7. If the glide slope became inoperative, could you continue this approach if established on the localizer at the time of the malfunction? Why? (AC 61-27C)

Yes, provided ATC is notified and approves a localizer-only approach. Since the procedure indicates a localizer-only minimum, a localizer-only approach can be authorized. The minimum is now an MDA and the approach is now a nonprecision procedure with MAP being a time or DME point.

8. If you discovered your marker beacon receiver was inoperative, what are the authorized substitutes for the MUFIN outer marker? (AC 61-27C)

Substitutes for the outer marker are:

a. The compass locator (365 kHz)

b. 5.3 DME I-FTW

c. DFW VORTAC radial 267

9. What DME distance is indicated in the profile view for the MUFIN LOM and the runway threshold? (AC 61-27C)

The MUFIN LOM is 5.3 NM, and the runway threshold is 1.5 NM from the localizer antenna site.

10. Where is the MAP for the precision and nonprecision approach in this procedure? (AC 61-27C)

a. For the precision approach procedure, the MAP is upon reaching the DH of 910 feet MSL on the glide slope.

b. For the nonprecision procedure, the MAP is:

    i. 1.5 DME from IFTW; or

    ii. Time from MUFIN.

K. Instrument Approach Procedure Charts: Minimums

1. What is the minimum visibility for a Category A full ILS 16L approach? (AC 61-27C)

Minimum visibility is $1/2$ mile or RVR of 2,400 feet.

2. If the approach light system became inoperative, how would you determine the minimum visibility for a Category A full ILS 16L approach? (AC 61-27C)

To determine landing minimums when components or aids of the system are inoperative or are not utilized, inoperative components or visual aids tables are published and normally appear in the front section of NOAA approach chart books.

3. Convert the following RVR values to meteorological visibility. (14 CFR 91.175)

1600	$1/4$ statute miles
2000	$3/8$ statute miles
2400	$1/2$ statute miles
3200	$5/8$ statute miles
4000	$3/4$ statute miles
4500	$7/8$ statute miles
5000	1 statute mile
6000	$1 1/4$ statute miles

4. Are takeoff minimums standard or nonstandard for Ft. Worth Meacham Field? (AC 61-27C)

They are either nonstandard or a departure procedure has been published, as noted by the symbol shown under the minimums box, which indicates that a separate listing should be consulted.

5. For the localizer approach 16L, what are the minimums for a Category A airplane if a circling maneuver is desired? (AC 61-27C)

The circling MDA is 1,260 MSL; the visibility requirement increases to 1 mile for the circling maneuver.

6. What significance do the numbers in parentheses (200 -$^1/_2$) have? (AC 61-27C)

Any minimums found in parentheses are not applicable to civil pilots. These minimums are directed at military pilots who should refer to appropriate regulations.

7. When established at the MDA on the final approach course inbound for the straight-in LOC 16L approach, is the MDA expressed as Height Above Touchdown (HAT) or Height Above Airport (HAA)? (AC 61-27C)

The MDA of 530 feet for a straight-in landing always represents height above touchdown (HAT) since the approach is for a specific runway. MDAs for circling approaches will always represent height above airport (HAA) since a specific runway will not be used for landing.

8. On what criteria are approach categories based? (AC 61-27C)

Approach categories are based on a speed of 1.3 x V_{S0} at maximum landing weight and forward CG.

9. **If the current weather reports indicate ceilings 100 overcast and visibility ¹/₂ mile, can a pilot legally make an approach to ILS 16L, and can he land?** (14 CFR 91.175)

Under 14 CFR Part 91, the approach may be attempted regardless of the ceiling and visibility. At the DH the pilot must have the runway environment in sight and have the prescribed flight visibility to land. If these conditions are met, the approach may be continued to a landing.

L. Instrument Approach Procedure Charts: Aerodrome

1. **What types of lighting are available for runway 16L?** (AC 61-27C)

HIRL — High-intensity runway lighting

MALSR — Medium-intensity approach lighting system with sequenced flashing lights; denoted by the circled A5 on the approach to runway 16L.

2. **What is the touchdown zone elevation for runway 16L?** (AC 61-27C)

The TDZE is 710 MSL.

3. **What is the bearing and distance of the MAP from the FAF?** (AC 61-27C)

The MAP is 164°, 3.8 NM from FAF for the localizer approach, and approximately the same distance for the full ILS approach.

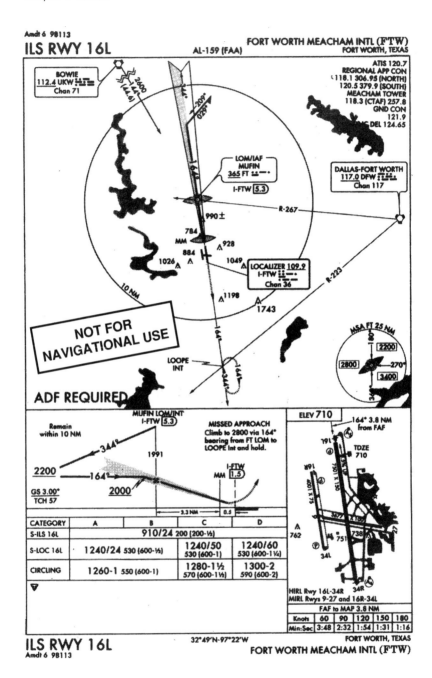

Notes

Notes